THE MONSTROUS REGIMENT

THE MONSTROUS REGIMENT

By CHRISTOPHER HOLLIS

"The Monstrous Empire of a cruel woman we know to be
the only occasion of all these miseries and yet with silence
we pass the time as though the matter did nothing appertain
to us."

JOHN KNOX: *First Blast of
The Trumpet against
the Monstrous Regiment.*

LONDON

SHEED & WARD

First published October 1929
by
SHEED & WARD
31 Paternoster Row, London, E.C.4
Second (revised) edition, January, 1931

CONTENTS

THE MONSTROUS REGIMENT

CHAPTER I

ENGLAND BEFORE ELIZABETH

ENGLAND was a province of the Roman Empire and became, by consequence, as did all the countries of Western Europe, a province of Catholic Christendom. She, of all Christendom's provinces, was the one least touched by heresy. She gave birth, it is true, to Pelagius, but the great mediæval heresies, which sprang from the attempt to dilute Christian theology with the thought of the Eastern and Mahommedan world, hardly penetrated to her. The Albigensian never reached her. An absurd phrase which has hailed Wyclif as "the morning star of the Reformation" only proves how extremely poor in English ancestry were the reformers of the 16th and 17th centuries and how very hard up for morning stars the Reformation was.

On the other hand, the English, while averse from theological speculation of any kind and instinctively hating heresy, were more vigorous than any of the Continental nations in their resistance to papal financial exactions. For this there are two especial reasons.

In the first place, the Papacy fell into the habit of discharging obligations to benefactors by a policy of "provisions," that is, by presenting those benefactors to sees, livings and prebends in far-off lands, which they never visited but from which they drew their revenues. This policy fell with particular hardness upon England and Scotland, the Papacy's most distant provinces. Secondly—and more important—during those years of the fourteenth century in which England was first learning from the French Wars to become conscious of her nationality, the popes, resident at Avignon, were politically the allies, if not the subjects, of the French kings. From the fourteenth century onwards, therefore, the patriotic Englishman's very orthodox Catholicism did not often err upon the side of a too great reverence for the person of the Pope.

Upon such an England fell the tremendous calamity of the Black Death of 1348, followed in the next century by the equally tremendous calamity of the Wars of the Roses. The old order fell and a new emerged. Mediæval society had been organised on the assumption that the priest was almost certain to be better educated than the layman. Many privileges had been granted to the priest which were justified not by his priesthood, but by his education. In the society which grew up after the Black Death the priests did not always have this educational superiority; yet many of them, being human, were unwilling to recognise the change of the times and to surrender their privileges.

In 1399 the ancient English monarchy was overthrown by a few rich men. To a superficial judgment that revolution seemed to have put into power a government more vigorously clerical than that of its Yorkist predecessor. In the reign of the first Lancastrian the defence of the Church by persecution was for the first time adopted as a normal policy of government. Yet the victory was the victory of clericalism rather than of Catholicism. Examine a list of thirteenth century archbishops, bishops or abbots. You will find from it evidence that the Napoleonic principle of *"la carrière ouverte aux talents"* was being applied by the Church of that date as it has never been applied before or since in human history. Examine such a list of fifteenth century dignitaries. You will find constantly recurring certain family names—Arundel, Beaufort and the rest. More and more during the Lancastrian ascendancy, the clerical "plums" came to be annexed by a few rich families who, while they professed to be defending the Church, were often defending little more than an economic arrangement, greatly to their own advantage.

The Church is unique. She is not to be compared and contrasted with other institutions. And whenever the mind allows itself to identify Her cause with some lesser cause—whether it be with an æsthetic movement or a social programme, with Conservative politics or with Labour politics—the result is always disastrous. For the Church is made to suffer for the sins of Her ally. Of all such identifications the most dangerous and the most false is that of the free Catholic society with a society in which a clerical oligarchy is allowed to regulate the every-day affairs of the secular majority —the identification, that is to say, of Catholicism with clericalism. The Church is a free society, in which the

priest, it is true, has an all-important function, but of
which the layman is as much a member as the priest.
He has his rights as much as the priest. His soul is of
equal value with that of the priest. The priest can make
no claims upon him save those which God has allowed
him to make in virtue of his office. Easy though it is to
misstate or misunderstand this truth, yet it is of the
very essence of Catholicism to insist upon it.

Nowhere can you find the menace of mere clericalism to Catholicism more clearly emphasised than in
that great mediæval, Catholic play, *Everyman*.

"There is no emperor, king, duke ne baron,"
says *Five-Wits*,
    "That of God hath commission,
    As hath the least priest in the world being;
    For of the Blessed Sacraments pure and benign
    He beareth the keys and thereof hath the cure
    For Man's redemption."

"If priests be good, it is so surely,"
agrees *Knowledge*, but adds that
    "Saint Peter, the Apostle, doth say
    That Jesu's curse hath all they
    Which God, their Saviour, do buy or sell,
    Or they for any money do take or tell.
    Sinful priests giveth the sinners examples bad;
    Their children sitteth by other men's fires I have
            heard;
    And som haunteth women's company
    With unclean life, as lusts of lechery.
    These be with sin made blind."

Campion himself said that the greatest need of the Church in his day was to bring to an end the rule of "ignorant ecclesiastics, simple preachers and old-fashioned monks." The Latin epigrams and English works of Sir Thomas More enforce the same lesson. The evil done by bad priests was large; all but as large was the evil done by the stupid, good priests. The evil of persecution was as nothing to that of these good men's stupidity. The full possibilities of a Catholic society will never be discovered until there shall appear one which possesses both an educated clergy and an educated laity. It is the tragedy of Europe that such a society has never yet existed. In the Middle Ages the laity was not educated. By the time that the laity had become educated the clergy had become corrupt. By the time that the clergy had reformed themselves, the laity had become irreligious.

To the throne of such an England, an England corrupted by the moral havoc of civil war, Henry VII forced his way in 1485. It was an England in which there was plenty of anti-clericalism (most of it combined with unhesitating belief in Catholic doctrine), the beginnings of scepticism, which had come in with the Renaissance, and hardly any heresy. There was too, in England, as in the other countries of Europe, a very evil confidence in clerical circles—a feeling that the unity of Europe, which had survived the scandal of the Great Schism, could survive anything and that therefore there was no need to bother with reform. There was also much genuine piety which was suspicious of the new learning of the Renaissance, and much equally genuine piety which was anxious to annex whatever was good in Renaissance learning, and to use it in order to make richer and deeper the Christian philosophy.

When in 1509 Henry VIII succeeded his father, no prophecy could have seemed more ridiculous than the prophecy that during his reign England would cast off her obedience to the see of Rome. Henry, an irreligious theologian, had at least all the normal Englishman's hatred of such chaotic speculation as was at the time being spread through Northern Germany. His desire for an annulment of his marriage with Katharine of Aragon, who had failed to give him a male heir, first caused him to threaten the Papacy with a repudiation of that authority which he had himself already admitted by his appeal to Rome. As Gray has put it in his cruelly satirical line,

"And Gospel light first dawned from Bullen's eyes;"

and Henry's sensitive conscience, troubled by the attractions of Anne, was unable to reconcile itself to the sin of continued marriage with a deceased brother's nominal widow. Henry found himself committed to action where he had at first only intended to threaten.

Yet he had no intention of doing more than transfer to himself that jurisdiction which had previously been exercised by the Pope. Indeed his discipline was stricter than papal discipline. As Bishop Stubbs wittily said of a later king, Henry as Supreme Head of the Church claimed to be "the Pope, the whole Pope and something more than the Pope." He made it a penal offence not to go to confession and said that celibacy of the clergy was not, as the Pope held, merely a disciplinary rule, but a law of God. In this he was clearly wrong, yet poor Cranmer, who had married the daughter of Osiander, the German Reformer, had to pack her up in a trunk as if she were luggage, in order to keep her dark. Henry wished for no accommodation with Protestantism, and was very willing to prove the impartiality of his mind by ordering that Protestants who denied Catholic doctrine should be dragged to the stake on the same hurdle with Catholics who persisted in maintaining the papal supremacy.

There was some opposition in Parliament to the first dissolution of the monasteries, but when Henry told the House of Commons, "I hear that my bill will not pass. I will have it pass or I will have some of your heads," opposition evaporated before the combination of greed and fear. There was one large rising against the changes—that of North England, known as the Pilgrimage of Grace. There are tales, too, of discontent among the poor, and a More or a Fisher was willing to lay down his life for the old doctrine. Yet on the whole Henry's policy seems to have shocked public opinion surprisingly little. There are several reasons for this.

First, Henry made no change of any importance in the ritual of the services or in defined doctrine. Quarrels between popes and kings were no novelty and the people did not understand that by this quarrel they had in any way been put outside the Catholic Church. Since the time of William I the kings of England had always possessed a larger power of ecclesiastical patronage than any other Christian monarch, and to most Englishmen the changes no doubt seemed nothing

B

more than a readjustment of relations which were continually being readjusted.

Secondly, the Renaissance' praise of the self-sufficient, strong man had led to an exaggerated and superstitious monarch-worship, which made people ready to tolerate, and even welcome, an arrogance of conduct in an occupant of a throne, greater probably than would have been conceivable either to any earlier or to any later generation. The New Learning had introduced a silly sneering at mediæval thought which the Renaissance knew only in its decadence. To the mediævalist good had always lain in the mean between two extremes. In reaction from this wisdom the Renaissance thought to find it in extremes. The Middle Ages tried to strike a balance between liberty and order. After the chaos of the Wars of the Roses, in England more even than elsewhere, men were willing to seek for peace at any price—even at the price of liberty—by submitting in all things to the despotism of a single ruler.

Thirdly, the development of artillery, which the strong, central government could afford but the local rebel could not afford, had smashed feudalism and strengthened the monarchies. Most men so wholly worship success that they very easily come to think that whatever is strong ought to be strong.

Fourthly, to the very crude nationalism of the sixteenth century there was something brave and patriotic in refusing to admit the supremacy of a foreigner.

Fifthly, there was the enormous motive of economic greed. Henry, it is all but certain, had no intention of making permanent the breach with Rome. There was no reason why that breach should not have been healed after the deaths of Katharine and Anne Boleyn, had it not been for the opposition of those who had profited financially from the change. It is important to understand clearly this capital point.

The money that used previously to go to Rome now remained in the country. Theoretically it was to go to the Crown, and Mr. Lytton Strachey praises the "cunning" of Henry in annexing those revenues to himself. Yet, in truth, he quite failed to do so. The new families were very well aware that they would be able to find means of steering that money into their own pockets. When to the papal dues was added the wealth of the monasteries, it became of desperate importance to this new, rapacious, unscrupulous, irreligious class that the old order should not be restored. The Church property was in theory, at least, public property, property held and administered by the monks in trust for certain public purposes. It was hardly more the personal property of the monks than the income-tax is to-day the personal property of the clerks of the Treasury. The practice, it is true, did not in the fifteenth century wholly conform to the theory, but it conformed a great deal more nearly than popular rhetoric is sometimes inclined to admit. Nor did the dissolution at all compel practice more nearly to conform to a theory of common use; it merely abolished the theory of common use. That is to say, by the dissolution this public property passed into private hands. Some estimate that as much as a third of the landed wealth of England changed hands, others say only a seventh. The true figure, which we cannot now discover, must lie somewhere between the two extremes, perhaps at about a fifth.

It is common to agree with the argument of Henry's creatures who, while admitting the existence of "divers great and solemn monasteries of this realm wherein (thanks be to God) religion is right well kept and observed," yet claimed that the smaller monasteries were hotbeds of corruption. Abuses there doubtless were, yet Cardinal Gasquet has adequately shown how completely unsubstantiated are sweeping charges of universal vice ; nor must it be forgotten that it was far safer to make accusations against the smaller monasteries, whose representatives were not there to defend themselves, than it was to attack the larger ones, whose mitred abbots were in their places in Parliament. Only later, when they had devoured the weak, did greed embolden the despoilers to attack the strong.

In Edward VI's reign the first attempt was made to give to the Church of England a definitely Protestant theology. The attempt was begun by one party under Somerset, a Seymour. Then, after Somerset had been betrayed by Cecil, the Secretary of his Council, it was continued by a rival but worse party under Northumberland. Cranmer had written one Prayer Book for Somerset, which he announced to have been "drawn up by the aid of the Holy Ghost." It would not do, and, on Somerset's fall, Northumberland made him write another in the composition of which he neglected to acknowledge the assistance of any such Collaborator.

"Do ye not know," explains one of the new grantees of the abbey lands of Sion in Sussex to his tenants, in the record of the Star Chamber proceedings of Henry VIII's reign, "that the King's grace hath put down all the houses of monks, friars and nuns? There-fore, now is the time come that we gentlemen will pull down the houses of such poor knaves as ye be." And the reign of Edward VI gave to "us gentlemen" a heaven-sent opportunity which they were not slow to take.

Somerset, a robber of the poor himself, had at least tried to protect the poor against the robberies of others. With Northumberland "the dance of all the dirt began." The Seymours were perhaps honest Protestants. If so, they were almost the only such among the new familes. A writer as little biassed against the Reformation as Macaulay has said that "of those who had an important share in bringing it about Ridley was perhaps the only person who did not consider it a mere political job."

The changes were intensely unpopular and were re-sisted by the people, as the changes of Henry's reign had never been resisted. In a letter (7th July, 1549), to the Protector Somerset, Sir William Paget, his chief secretary, admits that "the use of the old religion is for-bidden by a law and the use of the new is not yet im-printed in the stomachs of eleven of twelve parts of the realm." The resistance could only be suppressed by the introduction of German mercenaries. On the reason for this Burnet is surprisingly frank. "The bulk of the people of England," he says, "was still possessed with the old superstition to such a degree that it was visible they could not be depended on in any matter that related to the alterations that were made or were designed to be made; whereas the Germans were full of zeal on the other side." (*History of the Reformation.*)

We have the evidence of the reports of the Spanish, the French and the Venetian Ambassadors to prove to us that the great majority of the English governing class during these Tudor times was atheist. Many were atheist in open profession. More still were atheist in practice and betrayed their lack of faith in their jests and epigrams. Like the Earl of Arran, they "esteemed religion and worshipping of God but a superstitious terror to the consciences of the people to hold them in awe and obedience." Hell was "a bogle to flee bairns" and Heaven "but a conceit to make fools fayne." Cardinal Bentivoglio reports that four-fifths of the nation would declare themselves Catholic under a Catholic government, but that only one in thirty would demand Mass if the government were heretical. As Essex, the father of Elizabeth's favourite, said on his deathbed in 1576, "The Gospel had been preached to them, but they were neither Papists nor Protestants, of no religion but full of pride and iniquity. There was nothing but infidelity, infidelity, infidelity; atheism, atheism; no religion, no religion." The fools of each generation imagine themselves to have been the first to see through revealed religion. It is a great mistake, for their folly is more ancient than they think. At the bidding of the sovereign, writes the Venetian Ambassador in the reign of Queen Mary, the rich would declare themselves Jews or Mahommedans to-morrow.

Take as an example of the Protestant politician of the time the Duke of Northumberland, a man who cynically supported the Protestant cause during the vigour of his life and while it was to his economic interest to do so, but who, when he saw that the game was up and when the approach of death called him to more serious things, sought the consolations of the

Catholic Church. In words of some importance he exhorted the people "to stand to the religion of their ancestors, rejecting that of later date, which had occasioned all the misery of the foregoing thirty years." Himself, he said, "being blinded by ambition, he made a rack of his conscience."

The motive from which the governing class advocated the changes of Edward's reign was then not religious but economic. Early in the reign the chantries had followed the way of the monasteries. A small part of their income went to the maintenance of King Edward VI's Grammar Schools—which, as Mr. Tawney has explained in his *Religion and the Rise of Capitalism*, are not the schools which King Edward VI founded, but the schools which he did not destroy. A far larger part went into the pockets of "deserving noblemen." The next discovery was that Calvinism was an even cheaper religion than Henry's Anglicanism. It had been profitable to be rid of the Pope and the monks. It would be more profitable still to be rid of the bishops. These truths, which he doubtless held to be self-evident, that very pleasant and villainous courtier, Hobey, explained to the Protector (Jan. 19, 1549). He hopes "that the King's Majesty will appoint unto the good bishops an honest and competent living, sufficient for their maintenance, taking from them the rest of their worldly possessions and dignities and thereby avoid the vain glory that letteth truly and sincerely to do their duty." Having dealt with the bishops, he would have the Protector go on to the chapters. It would be a good plan, thinks Hobey, "if all the prebends within England were converted to the like use for the defence of our

country and the maintenance of honest, poor gentlemen."

For such purposes did the "honest, poor gentlemen"
of Edward's court use the small body of genuine reformers upon whom they could lay their hands. As a
result of "the King's godly proceedings" family after
family rose from nothing into plutocratic wealth, as
article after article of Church property was discovered,
like the plate of the poor minor-canons of St. George's,
Windsor, to be "fit for His Majesty's service and tending
to superstitious usages." The full accomplishment of
the courtiers' purpose was prevented by Edward's
death.

Edward VI was succeeded by his sister, Mary. The
new queen was welcomed with rapturous loyalty by the
people, and the attempts at treason against her were
easily defeated. Her religious policy was a double one
—to restore the old forms of service and to restore the
papal supremacy. In the first of these there was no
difficulty. The second had to be approached more
carefully. It had to be made very clear to the governing families that the restoration of the papal supremacy would not imply an attempt to restore to religious
uses the Church property which had been seized during
the last two reigns. Both the Pope and the Queen were
willing to give promises that the new owners should not
be disturbed, and the reconciliation of the country with
the Holy See was accomplished. It was welcomed by
the people, who were weary of the excesses of the last
two reigns.

Mary has left behind her an evil name in popular
history. The overwhelming majority of the country,

including Elizabeth, the heir to the throne, and almost the entire governing class, accepted the reconciliation. Yet there was a small sprinkling of genuine reforming fanatics, who, preferring, as it was reasonable to prefer if they were sincere, the interests of truth, as they saw it, to that of their country, persistently intrigued through the French Ambassador, Noailles, with the King of France, their sovereign's enemy, and with the Ambassador of Venice, the enemy of Spain. These reformers hated Catholicism and the priests. It was their purpose to rob the Christian faith of every practice or doctrine which implied a special priestly class. Against them Mary turned.

It is necessary to banish from the mind any picture of some gentle, slightly doddering country rector, summoned from his butterfly-collecting to the stake. There were, I do not doubt, such men among those who perished—men who suffered, as is the world's way, for the sins of their colleagues. Yet gentleness did not flourish easily in the extraordinary violence of sixteenth century Protestantism. The mild, well-mannered Laodiceans did not suffer from the Marian persecutions, for Mary did not burn people, as is sometimes loosely said, merely for not being Catholics. She burnt them only if they refused to admit any truth whatsoever in the Real Presence. "Is there or is there not anything taken and received in the Holy Sacrament besides Bread and Wine?" was the question put to the accused. It was a question which would have brought to the stake nobody who believed what was afterwards to become the doctrine of the Church of England.

A large part of the reformers—those who were

allowed to speak for the whole—were, as Gairdner has shown in his *Lollardy and the Reformation*, of the type that spits at the Blessed Sacrament, blasphemes against Our Lady and makes mock of the holiest things. To such a mind as Mary's, treason to Queen or country was a small matter beside an insult to the Sacraments. Therefore she did not persecute her enemies, as she might well have done, as traitors; she persecuted them as heretics. During her reign between two and three hundred, it seems, were burned. In merely secular justice Mary's rule was less harsh than that of her predecessors. Witness her reluctance to shed blood after Northumberland's first rebellion. To her reign we owe the important law that no one can be convicted of high treason except on the evidence of two witnesses. It would have been well if she had followed a milder policy in religion, too. Yet she preferred to believe with every sovereign of her time, of whatever creed, that it was her duty to compel her subjects to adhere to her own religious opinions. Nor is it unlikely that, as Froude suggests, she suffered during her last years from a touch of hereditary insanity which infected her judgment and goaded it into savagery.

Mary's violence fell for the most part upon the poor and ignorant fanatics. Cranmer, Ridley and Latimer were among the few people of distinction who perished.

Her blunder in equity was, that by punishing only for heresy she allowed the rich pilferers such as Cecil, the real villains of the piece, to slip through her hands. For they, of course, cheerfully conformed to Catholicism, as they would have conformed to Mormonism or fire-worship, if it had suited their purposes to do so.

Indeed, much of the most violent of the persecution came from men such as Paulet, the Marquess of Winchester, who accomplished the considerable feat of holding the Lord Treasurership from 1550 to 1572 without a break—from men, that is to say, who had been Protestant persecutors under Edward and were to become Protestant persecutors again under Elizabeth. As Dr. Storey was afterwards to lament, her vengance fell upon "the little twigs and shoots," but spared "the roots and great branches."

The sixteenth century was a crude and blood-spilling age, and it is neither probable nor proved that the persecutions were at all a large shock to public opinion. Bitterly though they differed from one another upon what constituted a heretic, there were yet very few people in England at that date who did not grant that heretics should in the last resort be burnt. Ridley, Latimer and Cranmer—all had burnt others when they had the chance. Mary's reign was rife with plots, and men were racking their brains for grievances which they could lay to the charge of her government. Yet they never complained of the fact that she burnt. They complained, it is true, that she burnt too much or that she burnt the wrong people, but they never complained because she punished for religious offences or because the punishment which she inflicted was the punishment of burning. Politically the burnings were a blunder, but not a very important blunder. That is to say, humane people disliked them and there were protests against them—especially from enlightened priests such as Alfonso de Castro, Philip's confessor. But the notion that the sight of these martyrs' sufferings in some way turned England Protestant is entirely baseless.

We must be careful of too easy agreement with tales of Mary's unpopularity. Much that appeared as hatred of her government meant in truth merely that the rich were in a panic lest she be successful. Certainly her popularity was declining during her last years. Still that decline was due, not to her religious persecution, but to the misfortunes of her foreign policy, to the economic distress, to the loss of Calais, and to the impression that she was allowing English interests to be subordinated to those of Spain.

Froude says that, if only Mary had been content to pursue a tolerant policy, she could have postponed the Reformation for a hundred years. The judgment is slipshod. For, in the first place, if she had postponed the Reformation for a hundred years she would have postponed it for ever. Only the most superficial of historical evolutionists can look on the Reformation as something inevitably bound to have come sooner or later. It is certain that if England had remained Catholic, the whole Protestant movement would have collapsed long before a hundred years were passed. The English State—and the English State alone—saved Protestantism. In the second place Froude, in recommending a policy of mere toleration, neglects the existence of a strong minority who were determined from the beginning of her reign to take every opportunity that offered, of making Mary's policy odious. This party was not, it is true, the party of the Protestant fanatics. It was the party of the *nouveaux riches* who knew that whatever the promises of Pope or Queen, an

England reconverted to Catholicism would never suffer the insolence of those who owed their power and wealth solely to their successful sacrilege. Mary's first blunder, as has been said, was not that she struck, but that she struck at the wrong people.

Her second blunder was her entire neglect of the Church's new triumph, of the great revived intellectual vigour of the Counter-Reformation.

Mary's religious policy, so far as it was genuinely unpopular, was unpopular not because it was Catholic but because it was Spanish. Men did not dislike Spaniards for being Catholics so much as they disliked Catholicism for being Spanish. The wiser of the Spaniards fully saw this. Charles V, her uncle, exhorted her to be " *une bonne Anglaise*," and the Spanish influence, such as it was, was always against a too vigorous persecution. The marriage arrangement with Philip was only agreed to on conditions so strict that there was no danger that Philip could ever become the master of England and so satisfactory that Elizabeth herself took them for the model for her own arrangements with Anjou. Yet treaties, though they could prevent Philip from being an English King, could not prevent Mary from being a Spanish Queen. While the Spaniards exhorted her to be English, Mary insisted on being Spanish, though even Spanish Mary, unlike her brother's ministers, never called in foreign troops to preserve her government from its English opponents.

CHAPTER II

ELIZABETH'S DECISION

In 1558 Mary died and was succeeded by her half-sister, Elizabeth. Throughout Mary's reign Elizabeth, if not herself engaged in conspiracy of treason against her sister, had at least been the candidate for the succession of those who were so engaged. Also—and it was the more important objection in Mary's eyes—though Elizabeth professed Catholicism and was loud in her protestations of sincerity, there was little doubt that she was really all but atheist, and would pursue whatever religious policy might seem to be to her convenience. It could not be very seriously held that she was legitimate, and the daughter of Henry VIII and Catharine of Aragon, at any rate, could hardly have been expected to admit that Anne Boleyn was Henry's lawful wife.

It may then seem surprising that Mary made no effort to prevent Elizabeth's succession. Elizabeth was as much an inconvenience to Mary Tudor as Mary Stuart was afterwards to become to Elizabeth. The elder sister had, it is true, more scruples than the younger. Yet it is possible that Mary Tudor would have solved the one problem in the way in which Elizabeth was to solve the other, had it not been for the influence of her husband, Philip of Spain. The Continent was at that time dominated by the conflict between the Hapsburgs of Spain and Austria and the French monarchy. It was important to Spain to keep England upon her side. But, if Elizabeth was excluded from the throne, the succession must go to Mary Queen of Scots, a French princess, soon to become the daughter-in-law of the French king and soon after that herself Queen of France. Philip, therefore, preferring his policy to his religion, supported the claims of Elizabeth, just as the King of France had preferred his policy to his religion in keeping alive the Protestant opposition to Mary. The reforming minority of the nation naturally enough felt that the accession of Elizabeth could not make their position worse and might make it better, while the policy of Philip assured the acquiescence of those who had been Mary's partisans. Elizabeth's ascent of the throne was therefore unchallenged.

The first question for her to decide was that of the religion which she was to favour. She had, as I have said, conformed to Catholicism and had professed great indignation at Mary's doubts whether she would continue her conformity when she became Queen. "I pray God that the earth may open and swallow me alive if I be not a true Roman Catholic," she had protested. She had pointedly sent no letter to the Pope on her accession, but at the same time in her letters to the Emperor and the King of Spain she professed the intention of honouring the promise which she had given to her half-sister. Yet she must not be blamed for her apostasy. It was not an apostasy in the sense in which, say, Luther's was an apostasy. For, though Elizabeth was for a time a nominal conformist, yet it is very clear that she never really had the Faith. Her nature was not such as to allow earlier promises to have much influence upon conduct; she had been brought up a Protestant and she soon showed her intention of reclaiming for herself that supremacy which her sister had given back to the Pope.

The best evidence upon her personal beliefs is that of the private prayers which were found after her death in her Prayer Book. They prove, I think, that she had a certain belief in God, if no especial belief in the Christian doctrines. For, wordy and ill expressed as they are, these prayers are presumably sincere. But for a chance they might well have never been seen by any other eye than hers. She could not have been lying to deceive others, and, if she was lying to deceive herself, there is no reason to think that she did not very completely succeed. I do not think that the author of these prayers can have positively recognised herself as atheist.

Yet for all that, though possessed of a certain talent for the production of conventional religious phraseology, she was certainly atheist in practice. Religion did not at all influence her conduct. This is admitted by both her friends and her foes, even if her friends sometimes cloak the admission by expressing it in some such phrase as that which says that she had "a mind superior to dogma." She had a contempt for the claims both of the Protestant and the Catholic religions—the greater contempt for the Protestant, if we may judge by her low opinion of her bishops and her dislike of a married clergy. A married clergy she could not, it is true, help herself but admit. Yet she only did so under the somewhat humiliating condition that the clergyman was

first to submit his *fiancée* to the inspection of the bishop
and two magistrates. Only after she had been passed
by them was she to be permitted to proceed to the
ceremony. "As for that necessary evil, their wives,"
runs a clause of a Bill of the Parliament of 1571. For
the Puritans, also, she had both contempt and distaste,
nor had she, at the beginning of her reign, any intention of entering into those relations with them into
which political necessity was afterwards to compel her
to enter.

For theological differences she had that scorn which
it is common to find in those who possess a certain
culture but lack any deep capacity for thought. "The
difference between Catholics and Lutherans was not of
much importance in substance," she told the Spanish
Ambassador. "All difference between Christians," she
said at another time, *"n'était que bagatelle."* "Many
people think we are Turks or Moors here, whereas we
only differ from other Catholics in things of small
importance." "The King of France and I both know
very well what religion the other holds and I believe
firmly that, though they differ in certain words, they
are not contrary in substance." "There is only one
Jesus Christ and one faith, and all the rest is a dispute
over trifles." Her theology was perhaps most adequately summed up by de Quadra, the Spanish Ambassador, who said, "It is all words." As Froude put it, its
technical terms "served to vary the vocabulary of her
oaths" and served, to her mind, for very little else.

If we consider how large was the part played by
religion in politics at that time, it is surprising to find
how very ignorant of theology the monarchs of Europe

were. "That a priest by muttering a few words could convert a cake into Almighty God had become for ever incredible," writes Froude, and even in the sixteenth century there were monarchs so ill-informed as to imagine such to be a just description of Catholic doctrine. And while on the one hand Philip of Spain as late as 1559 had to inquire and be informed that "this Calvin is a Frenchman and a great heretic," Elizabeth, on the other, was, we are told, quite surprisingly ignorant of Catholic doctrine.

So far as she had any œcumenical religious policy, that policy was to arrange a reunion of Christendom through the princes and without consulting the clergy— a policy which, had it not been for the vigorous Jesuit resistance to secular tyranny, was not ill-suited to that monarch-worshipping, anti-clerical age. Her ambition was probably less to appear as the champion of Protestantism than to hold the balance between Protestant and Catholic, as her father had held it between France and Spain, and Froude is very likely right in suggesting that not until very late in her reign did she come to look on her Church of England as anything more than a temporary arrangement, assumed for diplomatic convenience. Deficient in religious sense, she did not see that the unity of Christendom was permanently broken, until long after that break was apparent to many of her contemporaries.

There was no large popular pressure which demanded that she should overturn Mary's settlement. Why then was she not willing to let well alone?

A number of reasons seem to have combined to force her to her dangerous decision. In the first place, she was determined not to admit herself to be bastard. Now the Pope, although he might have been induced to recognise Elizabeth as Queen, could hardly have been expected to recognise her as legitimate. For she quite obviously was not legitimate. Even Henry VIII had declared it high treason to call her so, and a pope, of all people, could hardly be expected to deny Henry's marriage with Katharine of Aragon, the validity of which was dependent upon a papal dispensation. It happened, too, that the pope of the moment was Paul IV, a Neapolitan of the noble family of Caraffa, a violent hater of all things Spanish and, therefore, a supporter of the French view. It was this same Paul who had already gravely damaged the cause of English Catholicism by his unjust treatment of Cardinal Pole. Now the French naturally favoured the claims of Mary, Queen of Scots, their sovereign's daughter-in-law, and were therefore stout maintainers of Elizabeth's illegitimacy.

The power of England was at that time far from equal to that of Spain or France. "The sick man of Europe" Feria, the Spanish Ambassador, called England, anticipating by three hundred years a famous diplomatic phrase, and he warned his master that, if she was allowed to do so, France could with ease "take possession of this miserable country." Elizabeth could not then hope to be more than the fourth of Catholic princes. But the North German rulers who had embraced Protestantism were both petty and barbaric. If she could bring to Protestantism the great Roman province of Britain, she would be easily the first of Protestant princes. If she could hold it uncertainly

divided between the two faiths, she could compel her
neighbours to treat her as the central figure of European politics.

There were advantages in such a bold policy.
Though a patriotic Englishman might be ready to
admit Henry's headship of the Church, yet definitely
Protestant doctrine up till that time still had something
vaguely unpatriotic about it. During the sixteenth
century none of the great European nations save the
Spanish made a smaller contribution to specifically
Protestant speculation than did the English. Protestantism smacked of Geneva or of chaos, and the sound of it
was as foreign as, and more uncouth than, the claims of
papal supremacy. It had been, as I have said, the
German mercenaries who had preserved the Protestant
changes in Edward VI's time, and the Protestants had
done little to make their religion appear as an English
religion. They had been willing enough to admit that
God had laid upon them obligations which forced
them to become the enemies of their country, and
throughout Mary's reign they had been continually
at intrigue with the King of France, Mary's enemy.

As a theologian Luther was not of very serious importance. He had thrown overboard Reason, and all
controversy must cease when the controversialist repu-
diates Reason. There is nothing for it but the slanging
match. To this Luther had very readily taken, and his
last writings are hardly those of a sane man. The
leadership of living Protestantism had passed from the
chaos that was Luther to the lucid and energetic
French mind of John Calvin. Calvin alone had succeeded in opposing system to system and in seriously

challenging the Catholic theology. It still seemed just possible that he might succeed in capturing all France. It seemed certain that his followers would continue to have large influence over French policy. Protestantism at this date was looked on as a Latin rather than a Nordic business. France was the enemy of England, the friend of English Protestants. Elizabeth had at the least been sufficiently in touch with the treasons of those Protestants, from Wyatt's rebellion onwards, to be very well aware of their characters. It was all but certain that the King of France in his support of Mary, Queen of Scots, would continue against Elizabeth those intrigues which he had used against her sister. If Elizabeth declared herself Catholic, the French king would be able to use the English Reformers for his purposes. But if she declared herself Protestant, she could bolt that door against him.

Yet the English Reformers were, after all, but a small minority of the nation, and it may at first sight seem strange policy to conciliate a minority and, by doing so, antagonise the majority. But there was a great difference in character between the minority and the majority. The minority was fanatic. It admitted no obligation of patriotism and made it no secret that it would play the traitor to any government which did not favour its religion. Elizabeth had learnt from her observation in Mary's reign of the pertinacity of that party which would exploit every opportunity of discontent in order to make impossible the rule of Catholic government in England. On the other hand the majority, Catholic in sympathy, was composed of ordinary Englishmen. Now the normal Englishman of that date talked, it is true, a Catholic language. Yet, at the same time, he fell an easy victim to a patriotic spirit which he did not find it hard to confound with religion. He would be reluctant to oppose his sovereign if he were not forced to do so. Cecil, Elizabeth's minister, determined to trade on his patriotism.

Also, although England, so far as it had any religion, was Catholic, London was Protestant. It was the only place in England where priests had been openly insulted in the streets during Mary's reign. It was not certain that the support of London was not of more importance than that of all the rest of England.

Cecil had, too, another inducement to offer. To the atheist rich, a profession of faith had by now become little more than a commodity to be hawked about for a price. They were willing to swear anything, provided that, like Pooh-Bah in the *Mikado*, they were "sufficiently insulted." Mary, while keeping to her promise not to require the return of the Church land, had yet found means to relieve a little, out of her own pocket, the poverty of the Church. She had given to the Church the tithes and annates which in Henry's and Edward's reigns had been seized by the Crown. Cecil laid his hands upon all this money. He also passed an Act by which, on the vacancy of a bishopric, all that bishopric's lands, other than the manor-house and its immediate domain, were to become the property of the Crown, which was later to compensate the bishops for what it had taken. On Elizabeth's accession every one of the Marian bishops, except Kitchin, of Llandaff, was deprived of his see. The Crown thus acquired a reasonably substantial bribe with which to quiet the rich.

Cecil explained to Calvin that "if true religion is to be supported, it must first convert great noblemen." It converted some; others became great in the process of conversion. "Whether the revenues of these estates were now employed according to the intent and meaning of their donors, was a thing to be pondered and considered" decided the Parliament of 1571 with considerable humour.

Cecil's policy was simple in its purpose, however tortuous in its practice. From Elizabeth's accession to Cecil's death it had but a single aim—to decatholicise England. "Cecil's single principle is detestation of the Catholic faith," truly wrote the Spanish Ambassador to Philip. To decatholicise England meant not merely to break with the Pope—the breach with the papacy was but a detail, if a very necessary detail —but to expel the Mass from England. For, as long as people demanded the Mass, they would demand the priest. In order that Cecil and his friends might be safe in their stolen lands it was necessary to persuade people that they could get on well enough without priests.

The judgment is one which I do not think that historians of any school of thought would wish to question. The Catholic or the Protestant, as the words are normally used, will say that Cecil was successful. The Anglo-Catholic will, I suppose, say that he failed, that through all the changes the Church of England still preserved her Catholicism. But even the Anglo-Catholic must admit that, if the Church's Catholicism was preserved, it was preserved in spite of Cecil's policy and not because of it.

The only question was "Would the poor stand it?" or "Would they resist innovation as they had resisted it in Edward's time?" In the conditions of the sixteenth century it was not likely that the poor would act without leaders—and the leaders were bribed. Besides, Elizabeth's own main anxiety was to keep a precarious throne, and her masters, suspicious that, whatever guarantees were given, yet a Catholic England would never tolerate the rule of those who owed their power solely to successful sacrilege, determined that the breach with Rome and their share in the property which the Crown might have occasion to confiscate was the price for which they would serve her. Such were the reasons for Cecil's religious policy. It is in the nature of a shallow adventurer to despise the poor, and he determined to try the experiment. In 1559 the Acts of Supremacy and Uniformity were passed, and Elizabeth's headship of the Church was defined—in terms slightly more guarded than those which Henry VIII had used.

For these domestic reasons Elizabeth was compelled to the breach with Rome. To the Spanish Ambassador she confided, sincerely or not, that she was forced much further than she would have wished to go. What would Catholic Europe have to say? The foreign danger she did not greatly fear. For Catholic Europe was divided between the House of Hapsburg and the House of Valois. "To make a lewd comparison," said a contemporary Englishman," England is as a bone thrown between two dogs." It was not in human nature that the dogs should make a coalition together against the bone. Elizabeth felt confident that, whatever her domestic policy, Spain would always support her so long as Mary, Queen of Scots, was her rival. United Catholic action was only at all possible if Pius IV, the new Pope—Paul had died in August, 1559—should give a strong lead by an immediate excommunication of Elizabeth. By skilfully hinting to the Pope that Elizabeth was not yet finally decided upon her religious policy, Cecil persuaded Pius to hold his hand. During these fateful, first years the Papacy gave no lead to divided Catholic Europe, while those in England, who might otherwise have been Catholics, were allowed almost without protest to fall into the habit of attending the new Church services. The Papacy was out-manoeuvred.

CHAPTER III

THE BREATHING SPACE

No sooner was Elizabeth on the throne than there appeared a large number of suitors for her hand. Among these was the King of Spain, willing, as he condescendingly explained, "to do God a service" and marry Elizabeth. He demanded as his condition that she return to the Catholic Church. Elizabeth, doubtless, never had any intention of marrying him, but as was her habit she procrastinated. To her dismay Philip, instead of wasting his time, went straight off and married Elizabeth of France. The chances of a Franco-Spanish alliance, of which this marriage appeared to be the hint, were not even now very large. Yet Cecil was able to pretend that such an alliance was imminent, to persuade Elizabeth that the danger was desperate and thus to force her to do what she greatly disliked doing—to force her to paralyze the possibility of French effort by supporting the Huguenot rebels against the French king. Cecil, holding before his Queen the bait of the recovery of Calais, convinced her that, though she was officially on terms of friendship with the French kings (Francis II and Charles IX, who in 1560 succeeded his brother, Francis), yet her only hope lay in support of the Huguenots who were in rebellion against those kings. Thus and thus only could the civil war be prolonged and France kept permanently impotent.

The Government entered into intrigue with Antoine de Bourbon, the Protestant King of Navarre, and his brother, Condé. Throckmorton, Elizabeth's Ambassador in Paris, was sent to explain to Antoine de Bourbon "the esteem of the Queen for his virtues, her wish to form an alliance with him for the honour of God and the advancement of true religion and her hope that, by mutually assisting each other, they might prevent their enemies from taking any advantage against God, or His cause or either of themselves as His ministers." Which "true religion" was to be advanced, Throckmorton was not, it seems, instructed to explain, yet the matter was of some importance since Elizabeth's religion and Antoine de Bourbon's were quite different from one another. Indeed, they shared hardly anything except their common dislike of the Pope. It was enough.

The Duke of Guise one day charged Throckmorton to his face with being the "author of all the troubles" and Throckmorton did not deny the charge. Yet, Elizabeth, always stingy about money, demurred at the cost of supporting the Huguenots. Cecil, in an interesting memorandum, tried to frighten her by a highly coloured picture of the consequences to her of Huguenot failure. If the Huguenots were beaten, Cecil argued, the Guise faction, then dominant in France, would make an alliance with Philip of Spain, whose son would be married to Mary, Queen of Scots, now a widow owing to the death of Francis II. The two Catholic powers would proclaim Mary Queen of England, the Council of Trent would excommunicate heretic sovereigns and relieve Catholic subjects of their duty to them ; and Cecil bluntly told Elizabeth to be under no illusion — in the ensuing war all those in England who were attached to the old faith would take the side of Mary and the Catholic powers. It is no motive of charity or choice from which Cecil demands the support of the Huguenots and Dutch Protestants. It is a matter of life and death for him and for her. The Protestants must be helped, Cecil insists in a phrase which perfectly describes his policy, "first with promises, next with money and last with arms." He even wrings Elizabeth's consent to the organisation of a strong, secret offensive of which the purpose was to destroy the œcumenical character of the Council of Trent, which was to reopen in 1562. For this purpose it was necessary to induce as many princes as possible to refrain from sending their representatives. There was a price to be paid for such an offensive, necessary as it was. Because of it England was fast becoming the asylum of continental Protestants of every description whom Elizabeth's Bishop of London described as "a marvellous colluvies of evil persons, for the most part *facinorosi, ebriosi et sectarii.*"

Elizabeth's first experiment in favour of the Huguenots turned out quite disastrously. Though grudging the expense, she yet sent an army into Normandy in 1562. The only result of its presence on French soil was temporarily to unite the French factions in face of their country's enemy. The English army under the Earl of Warwick, isolated in Havre, was compelled to surrender in 1562. Calais remained, as it has remained to this day, in French hands.

Yet the problem of most immediate importance during these years was that of the policy to be adopted towards those in England who refused to support the religious settlement. All of the bishops but one had declined to take the oath recognising Elizabeth as head of the Church. The Universities had refused ; so had the majority of the higher, and some two hundred of the lower, clergy. Many more would have refused, had not the Government, unwilling to make too clean a sweep, practised wholesale connivance at the evasion of its own commands. Archbishop Parker was under instructions "not to push anyone to extremities on account of his oath." There had been as yet no general attempt to impose the oath upon the laity. It was uncertain what proportion among them would refuse it, but so little support had the Government's policy received that it was hard put to it to find Protestant gentlemen enough to fill up its benches of magistrates.

Cecil determined to have the whole question settled by the Parliament and Convocation of 1562. A Bill was presented to the Parliament by which the obligation to take the oath was extended to members of the House of Commons, to schoolmasters, private tutors and attorneys, to all persons who had ever held office in the Church or in any ecclesiastical court during the present or the last three reigns, but also to all who should openly disapprove of the established worship, or should celebrate, or hear others celebrate, any private Mass. A first refusal to take the oath was created an offence punishable by Praemunire. The punishment for a second offence was to be death.

There was some opposition. Yet the Bill, it goes without saying, passed through Parliament, just as any Bill for whatever purpose always passed through Parliament in Tudor times, provided that it had Government backing. Yet the debate in the House of Lords produced at least one brave and interesting speech—that from Lord Montague. Lord Montague began by saying that "it was known to all men that the Catholics had created no disturbance in the realm." He then went on to ask, with considerable ironic humour, whether the scriptural authority for the royal supremacy could be so entirely unquestionable, seeing that the claims of the Queen were claims not made by any other prince, whether Catholic or Protestant, anywhere else in Europe. Was it not possible that the Catholics who refused the oath of supremacy were at least in good faith? He concluded by a surprisingly frank statement of the real issue. He warned the House not to be intimidated by those "who looked to wax mighty and of power, by the confiscation, spoil and ruin of the houses of noble and ancient men." "What man," he asked, "is there so without courage and stomach, or void of all honour, that can consent or agree to receive an opinion and new religion by force and compulsion?" Sad experience was once more to prove that there were many such.

Convocation had met at the same time as Parliament. It consisted of those who had been recently restored or appointed to their posts, or of those who had kept them by taking the oath. The old Catholic priest, even if he was left undisturbed in his country parish, was naturally not allowed to associate himself with the deliberations of the Church. Naively the assembly began its deliberations by considering the question of an adequate provision for the lower clergy. Cecil and the rest of the courtiers, who had not robbed the Catholic clergy in order to endow the Anglicans, bade them pass on to the third question of their agenda —the important and harmless one of a promulgation of the beliefs of the Church of England. From these deliberations emerged an Act of Uniformity.

Superficially the new Church of England was a *via media* between Rome and Geneva—it had, for instance, less ritual than Rome and more than Geneva—and in some modern theories much is made of that superficial moderation. Yet in a more important sense its victory was the victory of the extremists and the Catholic way was, as it always is, the middle way. Against Calvin and Knox, who would allow to the prince virtually no rights at all, and Elizabeth and Luther, who claimed for the prince absolute rights over the Church, stood the *via media* of Catholicism, which both claimed freedom for the Church and also insisted upon an obligation of obedience to the sovereign—which insisted that the problem of politics was the difficult problem of finding the balance between the rights of the temporal and the rights of the spiritual —a problem which could only be ignored at peril.

While voting the Acts, Convocation wished to vote also penalties for heresy against those who refused to obey them. Cecil had already in the Act of Parliament a sufficient weapon either against Catholics or against

the Protestant preachers, if they should prove obstrep-
erous, and he had no intention of allowing to slip from
his fingers the all-important power of deciding by
what policy orthodoxy should be preserved. While he
fished in the troubled waters of Scottish Protestantism,
he was determined that in England new presbyter
should never become old priest writ large. The Scotch
Church was soon afterwards to succeed in imposing
upon the Regent Murray an oath "to smite all enemies
and heretics to the true worship of God that shall be
convict by the true kirk." But in England, persecution
was to be a government monopoly. "God keep us from
such visitation as Knox hath attempted in Scotland,
the people to be orderers of things," Archbishop
Parker was to exclaim with feeling and with sense.

The penal laws of Elizabeth must be contrasted with
those of Mary in three ways. First, Mary's laws were
directed to the defence of the normal Englishman's
religion, the religion which had been England's for a
thousand years, against the attacks of a small fanatic
party. Elizabeth's laws sought to punish with death
the profession of that faith, which until a few years ago,
at least, had been the faith of the overwhelming majority of Englishmen, which until a very few years ago
had been Elizabeth's own professed faith, to which she
had protested her sincerity with tears in her eyes and
which in her coronation oath she had sworn to support.
There can be no comparison at all between the proposition that a monarch has the right to persecute in
order to preserve a religion which has been the country's religion for a thousand years, and the proposition
that the monarch has a right to make up a new religion

according to her whim and to impose it by force upon her subjects. Cecil, in his defence, claimed that the Government only persecuted under "the laws of Parliament made in King Edward the Third's time, about the year of Our Lord, 1330." The claim was false, for it often persecuted under its own new treason statutes. But, even if true, it would not have been a justification. For the laws of Edward III were laws for the preservation of the religion of England, not laws for the preservation of a rigmarole which Edward III had made up as he went along. Mary, if she erred, erred with all her generation, but Elizabeth's was a new and an unheard-of insolence.

Secondly, Mary had at least honestly believed that the Catholic Church was the Church of Christ. No one seriously maintained that either Elizabeth or Cecil thought of the Elizabethan constitution as more than a political convenience, and Elizabeth probably thought of it as merely a temporary political convenience.

Thirdly, in Mary's reign the Protestants had already shown themselves to be ready to subvert the Government by treason, in the rebellion of Northumberland, in that of Wyatt and at other times. At the time of the passage of Elizabeth's Act, Catholics had in no way offered any opposition to the civil government.

Had Elizabeth really intended to enforce her Act with the supreme penalty the results would have been far more horrible than anything under Mary. It is only fair to her to say that she had no intention of doing so. To attempt it would have been folly and, I think, she quite genuinely did not want to persecute. Her hope was rather that, with such an Act upon the

D

statute-book, the Catholics would behave themselves
through fear, the atheists, greedy for their share of the
resulting spoliations, through hope, of its enforcement.

Cecil, on the other hand, though willing to persecute,
was not prepared for "bloody" persecution. It was
essential to keep the Pope quiet and to allow people to
get used to the new services—or rather, to get used to
doing without Mass. The time for bloody persecution
would come later. For the moment the laws were only
enforced when greed got the better of policy. "Some
think," ran the report of Bishops Grindal and Cox in
1562, "that if this priest, Harvard, might be put to
some kind of torment, and so driven to confess what he
knoweth, he might gain the Queen's Majesty a good
mass of money by the Masses that he hath said"—that
is, by revealing the names of those who had heard the
Masses, in order that such people might then be fined.

Since the death of her husband, Francis II, in 1560
and the murder of her kinsman, the great Duc de
Guise, in 1563, Mary, Queen of Scots, had been drifting
more and more away from a France, which, distracted
by its own civil troubles, could be of very little assistance to her in hers. More and more was she coming
to look to Spain as the one possible source of help.
For a time there was even a question of Mary's marrying Don Carlos, Philip's son—a marriage which might
possibly have come off but for the death in 1563 of de
Quadra, the master of the intrigue and Philip's
ambassador in London. Yet it could only have come
off in face of Elizabeth's opposition. To that and to
other schemes of foreign marriage Elizabeth was in-
telligibly opposed, and in the end Mary was married,

in 1565, to her cousin, Darnley, a weak and vicious fool but the heir to the Scotch throne. By birth he was the leading Catholic in Scotland, but his practice, or the lack of it, very plainly showed that his Catholicism was of a nominal and accommodating kind.

Into the tangled and interesting calamities which followed from that marriage it is beyond the purpose of this essay to enter. All history has record of few societies which were baser or more unpleasant than that of sixteenth-century England. But at least there was an intelligible sanity in the Elizabethan baseness. On the other hand, so confused and so filled with violence and vileness is the history of sixteenth-century Scotland that it is hardly possible to read it without thinking that one is reading the story of a nation of homicidal lunatics. Sadler, sent to Scotland as ambassador by Henry VIII, complained that "I think never man had to do with so rude, so inconsistent and beastly a nation as this is." It is hard not to agree.

In judging Mary we must then remember the society in which she was called upon to live. The causes which brought about the murder of Riccio in 1565—"most just and worthy of all praise" as Knox gleefully shouted— and the murder of Darnley in 1567, Mary's marriage with Bothwell, the rising against her, her forcible deposition, the part played in them by this or that politician—these are some of the most debated and some of the least solved problems of history. Even her stoutest defenders must admit that Mary behaved with very great indiscretion. Whether the Casket Letters be genuine or a forgery, there can be little doubt among any but the most impenitently romantic that the full truth, had it ever been allowed to come out, if it did not actually implicate Mary in the murder, would at least show her to have been guilty of some very doubtful intrigues. Discreditable to many other people, it would have been at least as discreditable to her. Lady Lennox, Darnley's mother, came at the end, it is true, to be persuaded of Mary's innocence. Yet the refusal to prosecute Bothwell, the Bothwell divorce, her marriage with Bothwell, her temporary apostasy—all these were the grossest and most flagrant scandals and were felt to be so even at such a time as that in which she lived. It is true enough that, however well she had conducted herself, her enemies would sooner or later have taken a chance to ruin her. When Darnley was still alive and no just scandal touched her name, the conspirators of the Riccio murder were certainly plotting to use her husband and his supposed grievances in order to drag her down from power. Yet it cannot be denied that by her conduct she gave these unscrupulous men an unnecessarily good excuse for doing what they wished to do.

Of the details of the parts played in these intrigues by Elizabeth and Cecil there is much room for uncertainty. Their broad policy is more clear. From his first accession to power, Cecil had consistently supported the Congregationalists, as Mary's enemies were called. After the fiasco of the expedition to Normandy Cecil abandoned the policy of open aid to Protestant rebels. His new plan was, whether in Scotland, in the Netherlands or in France, to cause Elizabeth openly to profess friendship with her Catholic fellow-monarchs, while he secretly supplied the Protestants in rebellion

against them with just sufficient support to ensure the
continuance of civil strife in their kingdoms. To the
rebels he excused himself for not giving more generous
help by complaining of the notorious stinginess of the
Queen. This policy he followed towards Scotland. As
early as 1559 the Spanish ambassador reports Elizabeth to be in intrigue with "a heretic preacher called
Knox."

The scandal of the Bothwell marriage deprived Mary
of her Continental supporters, and Elizabeth and Cecil
were clever enough to take advantage of the brief
breathing space. It would not, they knew, be long
before the adaptable consciences of the European courts
recovered from the shock. To take such an advantage
was very easy, for the scandals of ecclesiastical corruption in Scotland had been very gross, far worse than
those of England, as Catholics have freely admitted.

It is most important that we honestly face the truth
about the state of morality in Scotch ecclesiastical
circles. The hatred for Catholicism of a John Knox
was touched with insanity; yet it was not as wholly
lunatic as it appears to those who are ignorant of
the depths to which the Scotch clergy had sunk. Let
me give two instances where I might give many more.
Randolph, in his chit-chat on the progress of Scottish
Protestantism, writes: "They think to see next Sunday
Lady Stonehouse, by whom the Archbishop of St.
Andrews has had without shame five or six children,
openly repent herself." Again, Froude records that the
Bishop of Dunblane was popularly said to keep his own
daughter as his mistress. Whether the scandal was true
or false, its existence, at any rate, gives us a vivid

picture of the popular feeling of the laity towards the
clergy, and of popular opinion concerning the standard
of clerical celibacy. It proves, to put it mildly, that in
pre-Reformation Scotland that celibacy was to some
extent rather an ideal than a reality.

In Scotland, though Protestantism was by no means
democratic, yet at the same time Catholicism was
genuinely unpopular, and it was easy to raise a party
against a Catholic monarch. At first in Scotland, as in
England, the Protestant had been the unpatriotic
party; Protestant treachery had betrayed James V at
Solway Moss in 1542. But the French, Catholic rule of
Mary of Guise, Mary Stuart's mother, wise, cultured
and tolerant as it was, had yet made Protestantism
seem to be almost Scotch. Besides, the experience of
England had taught Cecil a piece of worldly wisdom
which he was very willing to hand on to his Scotch allies
and from which they were very willing to profit. Henry
VIII had sent Sadler in 1540 to explain to James V the
advantages of increasing "his possessions" by taking
from the monks such of their property as "might best
be spared." "Best be spared" by whom he did not
explain, and the Scotch king had unaccountably failed
to take the hint. But what the King had not understood
Cecil was now at pains to make clear to the nobility.
"In our first Reformation here in King Henry the
Eighth's time," he wrote, "if the prelatry had been
left in their pomp and power, the victory had been
theirs. I like no spoil, but I allow to have good things
put to a good end." The nobility showed themselves
to be more apt pupils than their royal master, and this
second hint was taken.

The nobles, having profited, were determined from the first not to allow Mary Stuart to obtain any real power in Scotland, just as the English rich had been determined not to allow Mary Tudor to obtain such power in England. Against such an array of opposition the wonder was not that Mary fell after five years, but that she lasted as long. Yet the chaos of these years reduced all Scotland to the extremity of barbarism and destitution. His responsibility for these conditions Cecil bore lightly. There was no starvation, he reported complacently, "except among the superfluous people." In order to justify its policy, the English government complained that Mary was intriguing with the English Catholics. The complaint was true, but Mary cleverly turned it to Cecil's confusion by arresting a certain Rokeby, nominally an English Catholic but in reality, as the examination of his papers proved, an *agent provocateur* of Cecil.

Elizabeth, though she lied about it, and lied badly, was yet very well aware that Cecil was supporting the lords in rebellion against Mary. Cecil, not the Queen, was the master of policy, and though Elizabeth disliked what Cecil was doing, she could not stop it. When in 1567 Mary was imprisoned by her enemies in Lochleven Castle and deposed from her throne Elizabeth was loud in her indignation. "Ill at ease with her escape from Holyrood and suffering from the sickness of pregnancy, she demanded to know whether the Queen of England intended to support the traitors who had slain her most faithful servant in her presence," Mary had asked in fine, scornful challenge after the Riccio murder. "If when at liberty you think fit to proceed against your opponents, in such case I will not fail to assist you," Elizabeth promised Mary. She made Cecil tell the Scotch lords that, "As I am a prince, if they continue to keep her in prison or touch her life or person, I will not fail to revenge it to the uttermost on such as shall be any wise guilty thereof."

There is no reason to doubt Elizabeth's sincerity. She genuinely disliked the dishonour of her own government's policy towards Mary and she had no love for the victories of rebels; these rebels also had been all too successful for her interests. To prevent Mary from getting too powerful was one thing; it was another to set up in Mary's place a strong, unpleasant, turbulent, aristocratic, Calvinist republic. The especial form of Knox' Protestantism, in whose name the Congregationalists had conquered, was a religion with which she was willing to have relations of friendship when it was necessary to do so, but to which she had personally a very great aversion. Knox himself she detested.

How far Cecil, her secretary, and Throckmorton, her ambassador, actually deceived Elizabeth concerning the policy they were following is uncertain. There was always intrigue within intrigue at the Elizabethan court, and the Queen, for all her fine Tudor bluster, was never her own mistress. In a moment of temper she once said to Cecil, "I have been strong enough to lift you out of the dirt, and I am still able to cast you down." How very far this was from being true is amply shown by her continual grants of land to Cecil and his friends. Cecil himself, for instance, collected, it seems, as many as thirteen estates. "The Queen's opinion is of little importance," wrote the Spanish ambassador in 1570, "and that of Leicester still less, so that Cecil unrestrainedly and arrogantly governs all." "Cecil, Sir Francis Knolles and their friends have gained her over," he reports again. "Cecil governs the Queen," and so on. Sir Henry Killigrew put the same point in a different way. "I know," he said, "that none can love their country better than Mr. Cecil: I would the Queen's Majesty could love it so well."

Cecil had at least succeeded in convincing the Regent Murray both of his own insincerity and of that of Elizabeth. "Although," Murray writes to Cecil with calculated insolence, "the Queen's Majesty, your mistress, outwardly seem not altogether to allow the present state here, yet doubt I not but her highness in heart likes it well enough. I have had infallible experience of your good will in especial." It is language such as might conceal many meanings. Both Murray and Cecil were very well aware that Elizabeth loathed "the present state here" like poison, but could not do anything to alter it. In England, as in Scotland, the nominal autocracy of a Queen was tempered by the real power of an oligarchy.

In the year 1568 Mary escaped from Lochleven. She raised an army, but it was defeated at Langside. Trusting to Elizabeth's promises of affection and support and in defiance of the advice of her wisest friends, Mary fled across the frontier and threw herself upon the protection of the Queen of England. Cecil had her seized, hurried quickly away from the Catholic borderland and thrown into prison in Bolton Castle. Mary's appearance on English territory raised a quite unfore-

seen problem. The best solution of it was anxiously debated at the Council. Elizabeth, if left to herself, would
have behaved honourably, and the later contradictions
in her conduct are due, I fancy, not so much to a
natural crookedness of character, as is often said, as to
the relic of a sense of honour, which was from time to
time breaking in on her, even as cheerfulness was from
time to time breaking in on the philosophy of Dr.
Johnson's lawyer friend, Edwardes. "The Queen,"
reported de Silva, the Spanish ambassador, "has
always shown herself favourable to the Queen of
Scots and now takes her part with the Council." Her
sense of honour demanded that she treat her cousin
properly, but it was never long before she was brought
back to heel by her masters, to whom Catholic Mary
was a danger in face of which Elizabeth's honour was
not to be deeply considered. Cecil's policy was to keep
Mary a prisoner for life and he was strong enough for
his policy to win the day.

Mary asked in indignant amazement why, when she
had come to ask for the redemption of a promise of
assistance, she should be treated as a criminal. If
Elizabeth would not help her, let her at least be
allowed to go her way to the court of some other prince
from whom she might beg help. It was answered that
she had asserted a claim to the English throne and
might perhaps assert one again. To her, as a Catholic,
all Catholics, both English and foreign, would be sure
to rally, and her liberty was therefore a necessary
menace to Elizabeth. Yet, though it is, of course, true
that Mary did style herself Queen of England—as for
that matter Elizabeth, like all English sovereigns from

Edward III to George III, styled herself Queen of France—yet since the death of her husband her immediate claim had been little more than a bargaining move, made in the hope of wringing from Elizabeth the recognition of the right to the succession. If the succession were granted, nothing more would be heard of the immediate claim.

Had Mary been merely left in prison, it would have been a cruel, but at least an intelligible, policy. To Cecil's mind imprisonment was not at all sufficient. She must also be discredited. Before the captivity Elizabeth had written to Mary, "Put yourself in my hands without reserve; I will listen to nothing which shall be said against you; your honour shall be safe and you shall be restored to your throne." Now for the first time Mary heard that an investigation into her conduct was to be held. Yet, to begin with, Elizabeth promised Mary that she should be restored whatever its verdict, and doubtless a restoration was what she wished for. But soon came Cecil's second victory and he caused Elizabeth to say that she was only willing to restore Mary to her throne if she could prove herself to be innocent of the charges of adultery and murder which were brought against her. "It was not meant, if the Queen of Scots should be found guilty of the murder, to restore her to Scotland, however her friends might brag to the contrary," Cecil now wrote. "We hear say," Elizabeth obediently chimed in to Murray, "that certain reports are made in sundry parts of Scotland that, whatsoever should fall out now upon the hearing of the Queen of Scots' cause in any proof to convince or acquit the said Queen concerning the horrible murder of her late husband, our cousin, we have determined to restore her to her kingdom; we do so much dislike hereof that we cannot endure the same to receive any credit. And therefore we assure you the same is untruly devised to our dishonour."

It was humiliating for Mary to have to submit to such an investigation into her private life. Yet, if she refused to submit, she knew very well that her refusal would be used by Cecil as if it were a confession of guilt.

Even to this day it is not certain who was responsible for the murder of Darnley. Nor does the question of Mary's guilt or innocence much concern this essay. It certainly did not much concern Cecil. Absence of proof does not necessarily argue innocence and there were plenty of suspicious circumstances. The Bishop of Ross' claim that "all the noblemen that heard her cause did judge her innocent" cannot be accepted in spite of Lingard's endorsement of it. Yet the attempt absolutely to prove anything against Mary failed. Nevertheless Cecil and Elizabeth knew enough of human nature to be very sure that if they threw sufficient mud some of it would stick. "I think that her acquittal should be so arranged that it should be left in doubt," Elizabeth told de Silva. Provided that he could discredit Mary, Cecil cared little if he also had to discredit his former friends in Scotland, such as Murray—friends who had by now served their turn. Cecil therefore in his report to Norris, the English ambassador in Paris, denies the Bishop of Ross' statement that the lords had thought Mary innocent. Elizabeth affected language of pity. "The circumstances produced to argue her guilt," wrote the Queen, "were such as we wished

that she and her commissioners had been otherwise
advised than to have entered so boldly into the treaty
thereof." At another time she claimed that "of her
indulgence" to Mary "she had suppressed documents
which would otherwise render her the execration of her
contemporaries and immortalize her infamy with
posterity."

Yet Cecil had raised up for himself enemies by the
bitter and violent part which he had played. A group
under the leadership of the Earl of Leicester, the
Queen's favourite, began to challenge his position in
the Council, and for a time he prudently confined
himself to his secretarial duties.

What was the policy of Leicester's party? Fénelon,
the French ambassador, in his reports to his master,
refers to this group and to those in the nation who supported them as "the Catholics." Cecil's party he calls
"the Protestants." He does not mean that the politicians who formed Leicester's party were people who
risked martyrdom every week in order to perform their
Catholic obligations. Many were, it is probable,
"Catholic Atheists"—to borrow the French term—that
is, people who themselves rejected the whole Christian
revelation but who, for one reason or another, thought
the political and social influence of Catholicism better
than that of Protestantism. There were doubtless some
who did practise their religion, and others who, in the
odd habit of that age, practised both religions simul-
taneously. It shows a misunderstanding of the tangles
of the sixteenth century to imagine that all who called
themselves Catholics imagined that they were under
obligation to refuse to attend another form of service

when it was prescribed by the state. Fénelon says that this party wished for the old worship. "They mean," as d'Espes, the Spanish ambassador who succeeded de Silva, explained to Alva, "to make an end of the present infamous government, to place the administration in the hands of Catholics and compel the Queen to go along with them. . . They say that they will re-establish the Catholic religion." At this time, as later in her reign, it was always taken for granted by both sides that, if the Catholics could only get hold of the government, they would have no difficulty at all in making Elizabeth declare herself Catholic.

If the Catholic religion was restored, these politi-cians, having restored it, would then have returned to their Catholic duties. They did not feel themselves bound to court martyrdom by attempting to perform them so long as the Protestants were in power. The responsibility for the unfrequented Sacrament they comfortably felt to be on the soul of those who had banished it from the land.

It is an error to think of Catholics and Protestants as divided from one another by a clear line as they are to-day. A small minority of the nation was determined to have Mass, whatever the cost, another small minority not to have Mass, whatever the cost. The great majority called themselves Catholics, but were Catho-lics of a very vague sort. To them the duties of a Catholic who was the subject of a heretical government were very imperfectly understood. Not until 1568 were the English Catholics definitely instructed that they must not attend the Elizabethan services. Even then the instructions were very imperfectly obeyed. For the moment the Catholics in the Council contented themselves with merely opposing Cecil's violent penal measures against those who did practise the old religion.

Of this party the Earl of Leicester was, as I have said, the leader. Yet Leicester, who now pretended that he was ready to swallow Catholicism in return for Spanish support for his marriage with Elizabeth, was later to jump from the devil of the Pope into the deep sea of Puritanism. How far he was at this time a crypto-Catholic it is hard to say. He was the son of that Northumberland who, it will be remembered, had made his dramatic confession of Catholic faith upon the scaffold; and he himself had been mixed up in more than one tortuous intrigue with de Silva to whom he had professed crypto-Catholicism. But he was intriguing with French Huguenots at the same time that he was intriguing with de Silva, and in personal belief he was most probably atheist throughout. Yet, though the leader for immediate purposes, he was not, says Fénelon, in the confidence of his party concerning their ultimate designs.

For the moment it was the policy of these "Catholics" to right the wrong which they felt to have been done to Mary, Queen of Scots, and by so doing to ensure the country against a renewal of the Wars of the Roses should Elizabeth suddenly die. The Tudors were a short-lived and unhealthy race. Elizabeth had nearly died in 1561, and general opinion did not expect her to survive many years. The notion that she might live on into the seventeenth century would have seemed almost beyond possibility. The wish of the "Catholics" was then to marry Mary to the Duke of Norfolk, to restore her to her throne of Scotland, to substitute for the Scotch Calvinism a Church on the model of the Church of England and to cause Mary to be recognised as Elizabeth's successor.

The objections of Cecil to such a policy are easily understood; he had no intention of ever allowing Catholic Mary to succeed. But it might seem that there was no reason why Elizabeth should disapprove of it. Yet Elizabeth had always the greatest dislike of any discussion of the question of her successor. Partly this dislike came, it seems, merely from a selfish and morbid repugnance to anything which reminded her of her mortality—a repugnance that was so strong that she preferred to endanger her own life rather than make any settlement of what should happen after her death. But it had, too, a more sensible cause. If she had been capable of doing so, it would have been enormously to her advantage to have had a child, but she was all but certainly incapable. There remained, therefore, the question of her successor.

Once the problem of the succession was settled, the courtiers, she said, would all flock "from the setting to the rising sun." They would desert her and reserve their flatteries for whoever was to succeed her. As long as the question remained unsettled, all the claimants would be likely to support her from the hope of obtaining her suffrage. Right up to the time of the Bull of Deposition and even after the scandal of the Darnley murder it is probably true that Elizabeth, knowing that she could not herself bear a child, intended that Mary should be her successor; but she did not intend formally to recognise her as such. Sane and moderate opinion also supported Mary's right and, what is more, wished Elizabeth formally to recognise it. Cecil and his party were determined that Mary should never succeed.

Cecil was therefore easily able to arouse Elizabeth's displeasure. The Duke of Norfolk, who had certainly been engaged in shady intrigue with Spain, was cast into the Tower, and the other leaders of the party were either excluded from her presence or else placed under arrest. Among them was one, Ridolfi, an Italian banker, who had been settled in England for fifteen years and who acted, it was afterwards to be discovered, as a secret agent of the Pope.

Often the only result of punishing the moderate members of a party is to throw power into the hands of its extremists. So it was now. The Catholic party of the north of England was by no means content to pursue its ends by cabinet intrigue and diplomatic feint, by winning a concession here and by discrediting an opponent there.

Nothing could be more false than the common notion that the Elizabethan settlement had been tamely accepted by all but a few malcontents. Throughout all England one effect of it had been to leave a large proportion of the churches deserted of any incumbent. Prebends were handed out wholesale to laymen. Camden, the antiquary, for instance, though he was never in orders, yet held the prebend of Ilfracombe from 1589 until his death in 1623; and we shall find Topcliffe, the torturer, and Sir Christopher Wray, the Lord Chief Justice, fighting one another over a stall in Lincoln Cathedral. Even of the bishoprics

E

Ely stood vacant for eighteen years, Chichester, Bristol, Worcester, Bath and Wells and Salisbury for periods of from three to ten years, Oxford for forty-one out of the forty-five years of Elizabeth's reign. Where the sees were filled, the incumbents were often so little suitable that it would have been almost as well to have left the vacancies. Archbishop Grindal's Memoir on Archbishop Parker, if unfair in the personal charges which the Primate made against his predecessor, adequately shows that in general the financial corruption of the pre-Reformation was fully maintained by the post-Reformation clergy; while, when the Archbishop of York was found in bed with an innkeeper's wife at Doncaster and defended himself with the somewhat unconvincing explanation that she had got in without his noticing it, it was evident that the sexual problems of clerical life had not been wholly solved by the mere abandonment of a rule of celibacy. William Rufus was a conscientious ecclesiastical patron in contrast with Elizabeth. Neither the Queen nor the courtiers objected to the vacant sees, for they, of course, shared the revenues between them. In many Churches neither Mass nor the Common Prayer was ever said, and report after report from the Bishops, such as there were of them, bears witness to the difficulty of enforcing the new order. Archbishop Parker had to be warned, as I have said, "not to push any one to extremities on account of his oath." "Being 13,000 parishes," pleaded his successor in 1585, "I know not how this realm should yield as many learned preachers." "Jesus," quoth the Queen, "13,000 is not looked for. I think the time has been there hath not been four preachers in a diocese."

What was difficult in the South of England was impossible in the North. "God's glorious Gospel could not take place," complained the Bishop of Carlisle. "The few Protestants that there were durst not be known for fear of a shrewd turn." Magistrates who would enforce the law could not be found. There were "wishings and wagers for the alteration of religion" and "rumours and tales for the Spaniards and the Frenchmen to come in for the Reformation of the same." In the North there had not been resistance to the settlement only because no very serious attempt had been made to enforce it in any but the main and most accessible places. "Religion was backward" in the language of the Government. "There are not," reports Sadler, Elizabeth's secretary, "in all this country ten gentlemen that do favour and allow of Her Majesty's proceedings in the cause of religion."

Since the passage of the penal laws, by which every Catholic life was nominally forfeit, it could hardly be pretended that there was any more obligation on an English Catholic to be loyal to Elizabeth than there was on a Mexican Catholic to be loyal to Calles' government in that country. If he tolerated the government, he tolerated it from expediency and not from duty. If he refrained from rebellion, it could only be from motives of prudence or fear. Now the news of the Duke of Norfolk's arrest and of the attack upon their friends in the Council convinced the two great Catholic noblemen of the North, Percy of Northumberland and Neville of Westmorland, that their only hope lay in desperate remedies. They would perhaps even now have willingly escaped the responsibility of rebellion, but they had committed themselves so far that "returning" were as dangerous as "go o'er." In this year of 1569 they attempted to raise the North against the Government.

The military details of the rebellion are beyond the purpose of this essay. That it failed is certain ; the reasons why it failed are less certain. It suffered, first, from a scarcity of leaders. The gentry, the natural leaders of insurrection, had been bribed with abbey lands. It suffered also from the too common handicaps of a rebellion, incompetent leadership and quarrels between rival leaders, such as they were. The leaders, who were of the old nobility, showed themselves to be at least as much concerned with chastising the insolence of the *nouveaux riches* as with restoring the old religion. In the northern rising, as later in the seminaries and as through all the last chequered three hundred years of its history, English Catholicism was cursed with its besetting sin of snobbery. Yet it is only fair to remember that in the sixteenth century neither on the one side nor on the other was there any idea of social equality, and that the Catholics, when they boasted that the old families were on their side, meant no more than that they were supported by the few among the rich and educated who had not made their money out of the loot of the monasteries and who were therefore capable of an independent opinion—by what Grattan was afterwards to call "the unbribed intellect of the nation." Yet a religion which is reduced to boasting of such irrelevant nonsense as the ancient lineage of its ad-herents is a religion already half defeated.

We condemn, and rightly condemn, the Reformation

as the ramp of the *nouveaux riches*. Yet it is in nature that old aristocracies should die and new aristocracies should replace them. The old mediæval society had been a closed society. The discovery and colonisation of the new lands, Europe's bursting of her old bonds, must inevitably have led, even without any religious complication, to a redistribution of wealth. The overthrow of religion was not wrong merely because it went hand in hand with a change in the ownership of English land. Rather was the change wrong because it went hand in hand with the overthrow of true religion—with an overthrow of all morals—because it was accomplished by vileness and preserved by violence. If the cause of the Reformation was little more than the defence of the *nouveaux riches*, that of Catholicism was a great deal more than the defence of the *anciens riches*.

The northern rising suffered from other misfortunes. The Spanish help which d'Espes, the ambassador, promised was not forthcoming. Dr. Nicholas Morton, the Pope's envoy, encouraged the North to rise by announcing that the Pope had issued a Bull of Deposition against Elizabeth. There was a muddle about publication and the Bull had not yet been issued. When it was discovered that Morton's claim was not true, it was suspected that all his promises of papal support were equally fallacious.

Moreover, the leaders of the insurrection were in a difficulty. Mary, Queen of Scots, was Elizabeth's prisoner. If they openly proclaimed her as Queen, there was every likelihood that Cecil would force Elizabeth to kill her. They had therefore to content

themselves with proclaiming that Elizabeth was surrounded "by divers new set-up nobles, who not only
go about to overthrow and put down the ancient
nobility of the realm, but have also misused the Queen's
Majesty's own person, and also have by the space of
twelve years now past set up and maintained a new-
found religion and heresy, contrary to God's word."
The freeing of Elizabeth from her own headship of her
own Church was an odd cause in which to take up
arms. A rebellion that fights on a compromise is rarely
successful.

The rebellion was not defeated. It frittered away,
and Percy and Neville fled to Scotland. Thither
Leonard Dacre, who rose soon after the earls, soon
after followed them. Cecil had been careful to keep
himself out of the way on a plea of sickness during the
critical time. It was a game which he was in the habit
of playing. He had played it before at the time of the
proclamation of Lady Jane Grey, but they had then
told him that he was shamming and had forced him to
sign the instrument devising the succession to Lady
Jane. This he did, though he afterwards betrayed his
confederates and lied about it. So now, recovering his
health as soon as he heard of the failure of the rebellion,
he wrote to Norris, the ambassador in Paris, that
Elizabeth "hath had service readily of all sorts without
respect of religion," but this was doubtless an exaggeration to be served out to the French king, in order
to persuade him that it was not worth his while to
reply to Elizabeth's intrigues with the Huguenots by
counter-intrigues with the Catholics in the north of
England. The truth seems to be that even the loyalty

of Sussex, the Lord President of the North, who, as Elizabeth's deputy in Ireland, had badly bungled his business of hiring assassins for Shane O'Neill, was itself at the least gravely suspect and that he was very commonly thought to be waiting to see which side was going to win before declaring himself. His half-brother, Egremont Radcliffe, was out with the rebels and he himself had been until Elizabeth's accession a professing Catholic. The sympathies of his army with the insurgents were so outspoken that he did not dare to give battle, and, when the insurgents attacked Elizabeth's other army at Barnard Castle, it mutinied "so far as in one day and night 226 men leaped over the walls and opened the gates and went to the enemy." Sadler is doubtless speaking the truth when he draws a distinction between the leaders of the insurrection and their cause : "I find the gentlemen of this country, though the most part of them be well affected to the cause which the rebels make the colour of their rebellion, yet in outward show well affected to serve Your Majesty truly against them," he reported.

As soon as the rebellion was over, Cecil, as has been said, recovered of his illness and entered with zest into the task of parcelling out the property of those who had taken part in it. Sussex, too, as though very anxious to silence all doubts of his loyalty by the atrociousness of his vengeance, joined in the work. The property of those insurgents who possessed any was seized in order to pay the expenses of the suppression and also to provide "a fund of remuneration for the services of her"—Elizabeth's—"adherents." The only difficulty concerned the lands in the diocese of Durham. Since the bishop was a prince-bishop, did not forfeited lands by right fall in to him rather than to the Crown? It was suggested that the bishop should be transferred to another see and that the Crown could then legally annex the forfeits on the ground of the see's vacancy. But eventually the law authorities obediently ruled that "by the 25th of Edward III's all forfeitures of escheats in all circumstances and all places belonged to the Crown." Only Lord Hunsdon urged that the Queen should "more regard her honour than her purse"—a point of view that to both Elizabeth and Cecil appeared as paradoxical as it was comic.

A terrible vengeance was taken on the landless. "We do marvel that we have heard of no execution by martial law, as was appointed, of the meaner sort of rebels in the North. If the same be not already done, you are to proceed thereunto for the terror of others, with expedition to certify us of your doing therein," wrote Elizabeth to the Earl of Sussex. "I guess that it will not be under 6 or 7 hundred at the least that shall be executed of the common sort," answered loyal Sussex, "besides the prisoners taken in the field." The poor, flogged people were left in a state of mad desperation. "Some few of them suffered," Cecil is constrained to admit of this, the most appalling of all the official butcheries in English history. Of all forms of government, government by panic is the most brutal.

There is a sense in which the northern rebellion may be said almost to mark the end of English history. I remember the old schoolboy version of the Elizabethan times—the proud Virgin Queen, lover of England, brave sea-dogs, gallant courtiers, wise statesmen, a nation which was feeling the first stirrings of its greatness, the whole world a young man's world. Put beside it another picture. A poor, weak, badgered Queen—a gang of crooks, who by a dirty chance had made themselves masters of England and the Queen, and who were playing a desperate and panicky game in order that they might be able to keep that which they had pillaged in sacrilege—the rich atheist, the poor, starving and landless—God banished from English altars, and the gallows of three counties creaking with the corpses of the last men who have died for English freedom. Is not the second picture at least as nearly true as the first?

Of those who were executed only two—Percy himself and one, Plumtree—are technically classed as martyrs. These two were offered their lives on condition that they apostatised, and they refused to do so. The rest are judged to have died in a political cause. Yet, if a government makes death the penalty for the practice of religion and then executes those who revolt against its authority, the plea that it kills them as traitors is little more than verbal. Elizabeth issued a proclamation denying "an intention of persecuting for religious opinions," and went on to promise that she would harm none, "as long as they should outwardly conform to the laws of the realm." Her promise was a promise that she would respect hypocrisy but would not respect sincerity. For a promise of freedom of conscience, even without freedom of worship, may be of value to those who think that the external acts of worship are indifferent. It is no concession at all to the

Catholic, whose conscience imposes upon him the obligation of attendance at a particular form of worship. Nor did the promise in the least mean, as is sometimes thought, that people would be allowed to do what they liked provided that they kept their practices to the secrecy of their own houses. A vigorous campaign of the ransacking of private houses for evidence of "private superstitious devotions," such as Latin Prayer Books or *Agnus Deis*, was instituted. Enforcement, as I have admitted, was erratic and partial. Yet if much "superstitious devotion" escaped the keen eye of the commissioners, that was due entirely to their lack of power and not at all to their good will.

As long as Pius IV had been on the throne he had followed the policy of making Elizabeth's reconciliation with the Holy See as easy as possible. There had been attempts at negotiation—first, with one Parpaglia, and then with Abbot Martinengo. With Martinengo Elizabeth would perhaps have negotiated if Cecil had not prevented her. In 1565 Pius IV had died. His successor, St. Pius V, was for a more aggressive policy. He therefore issued a Bull, deposing Elizabeth, releasing her subjects from their obligation of obedience, and calling on all Catholic princes to join in removing her from the throne.

The Bull was a blunder, as Urban VII afterwards admitted* and indeed as St. Pius is said to have admitted himself. Just as immediately after the last war many people thought that the powers of Europe should

---

*Over a suggested excommunication of the then King of Sweden, see Dom Norbert Birt's *The Elizabethan Religious Settlement*.

unite in a crusade to free Russia from the Bolsheviks, so it was arguable that at this date the princes of Europe ought to unite to free England from Cecil and his party. There was much sense in Nicholas Saunders' contention that "the state of Christendom dependeth upon the stout assailing of England," or in the reflection, "What glory it would be by winning back England to rob the nest of heresy, to purge France and Flanders and give an example to Germany." With the collapse of the English Government all Protestantism would have collapsed. Yet it is useless to threaten where you cannot perform. The question was not what Catholic Europe ought to do, but what it could be induced to do. Through incompetent organisation the opportunity of the Rising of the North was missed. It was certain that the Kings of Spain and France would not be willing to unite on such a common crusade, while the Emperor was unable to act since his hands were already more than full with the menace of the Mahommedan. Nor was either Most Catholic king, Most Christian king, or emperor, at all anxious to encourage in the Papacy the use of a power which might one day be invoked against himself. Without the support of these princes there could be no crusade. St. Pius, an unworldly saint, was ill-informed concerning the political conditions either of England or of the Continental Catholic countries. The chief effect of the Bull was to give Cecil a colourable pretext for his policy of persecution at home and of piracy and support of rebellion abroad. Nor were things made better when the blunder of St. Pius was repeated by his successor, Gregory XIII, in his support of the disastrous Irish expedition of 1579.

Cecil's policy was, as has been explained, to keep France and Spain incapable of any great action by the steady, but small, support of their Huguenot and Netherland rebels. To the complaints of the French and Sp nish ambassadors he could from now onwards always reply by pointing to the obligation which St. Pius had laid upon all Catholic princes.

St. Pius' Bull was then, as I have admitted, an enormous blunder. Technically, too, it was uncanonical, since by canon law a year had to elapse between the excommunication of a sovereign and his deposition. But the action of the Pope, though it was foolish and inexpedient, was certainly not, on broad grounds, *ultra vires*. The servile and decadent political philosophy of the day was busying itself, both in Catholic and non-Catholic countries, with arguing that the rights of the sovereign over the subject were unlimited. "My wisest clergy maintain on the authority of Holy Writ that no rising against one's prince, not even for conscience' sake, can be just and reasonable," Elizabeth told Fénelon. No doubt they did; they would not long have remained her "wisest clergy" had they not done so. Yet it is impossible not to regret that the relevant passages from which they drew their argument should so unaccountably have escaped the attention of Elizabeth's grandfather on the day of the battle of Bosworth. To such Oriental doctrine the best minds of free Europe have never submitted, and even in Elizabeth's own low day the sovereignty of the people was being preached in France by the Huguenot, Duplessis-Mornay, while on the Catholic side the cause of freedom was upheld by the Jesuits, notably by Robert Persons among Englishmen, and by the great Suarez among Spaniards. James I's pretensions were soon to be questioned on the same ground by the logic of Bellarmine.

"When you are unjust, the deity,
  Which you may challenge as a king, parts from you,"

taught Massinger in the *Maid of Honour*. The cause of these great men was the cause of common sense.

Elizabeth's rights were not absolute. All the best European minds from St. Anselm to Rousseau and De Maistre have held that under no circumstances can one soul possibly have absolute moral rights over another. There must come a point at which the right to obedience is forfeited. Even in the Jesuit rule, the inferior is under no obligation to obey the superior, if the order given is sinful, nor, as Richard Shelley told Elizabeth, can the Pope order a Catholic to commit a sin. In the old argument of the common law, which was used against Elizabeth by Catholic barristers, such as Plowden, two generations before it was used by Parliamentary barristers against Charles, the King of England was *sub Deo et lege*. He was not irresponsible. In trial after trial the Crown lawyers, unable to prove that the defendant had committed treason, would try instead to wring from him an admission that under certain hypothetical circumstances he might commit treason. The answer of the defending barrister was that, if treason were what the Government defined it as being, under certain circumstances any sane man would commit treason against any government.

And, whatever be the truth of the general speculation concerning an unspoken contract at the basis of every society, there certainly was, as it happened, a spoken contract at the basis of Elizabethan society. Elizabeth had received her crown on the condition of her coronation oath, in which she had sworn, among other things, to maintain "the liberties of the established Church and the laws, customs and privileges granted to the clergy by her predecessor, St. Edward the Confessor." The established Church, at the time of that oath, was the Church of Rome, and whatever might be the argument of a sincere Anglican, a Catholic at least could hardly deny that she had violated her oath— had violated, that is, the condition upon which he owed her his allegiance.

There is something quite comically one-sided about the version of English history which is to-day commonly taught in English schools. According to this view, rebellion against a monarch at any time previous to the sixteenth century was admirable and freedom-loving and Whiggish, and rebellion in the seventeenth century had again become admirable and freedom-loving and Whiggish, but rebellion against Elizabeth and the Elizabethan settlement was, on the other hand, unpatriotic and of the devil. In the same way it was pardonable both in the barons of Magna Charta and in the plutocrats of 1688 to have called the foreigner into England, but it was unpardonable in the Catholics of Elizabeth's reign.

That the Catholic was under no obligation to obey

Elizabeth is then beyond argument. The only question is whether it was any business of the Pope to declare him free from that obligation. Much ink is wasted in denouncing the tyranny of the papal claims in the belief that the deposing power, claimed by St. Pius' Bull, was the power which Innocent III claimed—a power of unlimited interference in secular affairs. The deposing power, it is true, was clearly defined by the Lateran Council of 1215 when Innocent was on the papal throne. Yet St. Pius was only claiming to exercise a power much more definite than that which had been granted to Innocent III. He was not saying: "You are a very bad king; therefore I declare your throne forfeit," or, "You are a Protectionist; I happen to be a Free Trader, so off you go." His argument was, "Elizabeth holds her throne from God on certain express conditions. Her oath was a religious oath taken before God's altar. As the Vicar of God, I therefore claim the right to say when those conditions have been violated."

If the Pope is the supreme authority within the Catholic Church upon faith and morals, then it obviously falls to the Pope, in the last resort, to say when there has been committed such a breach of morals as is implied in the violation of an oath. The power is not verbally specified, it is true, in Our Lord's commission to St. Peter, but, as Blessed Edmund Campion argued, the Pope's *ordinata potestas*, or power assigned to him *totidem verbis*, obviously carries with it a certain *inordinata potestas* to be naturally deduced from it. The only alternative to a Papal decision is that the individual should decide for himself. This the individual is often unable to do; it is offensive if he does it, nor is it fair to the sovereign, who is one party to the contract, that the decision whether the contract has been broken should be left entirely in the hands of the other party to it. Again, the lover of nationalism may argue that such a decision should come most properly from the national ecclesiastical leaders, but whose fault was it that in Elizabeth's time there were no national ecclesiastical leaders capable of giving such a free decision?

The Church has always insisted that man has a temporal as well as a spiritual allegiance, but since all obligation must primarily be an obligation to God, to Whom alone we are under obligation, and since we have an obligation to man only in virtue of, and as a part of, our obligation to God, the spiritual, as De Maistre showed in his day, and as M. Maritain has shown in ours in *La Primauté du Spirituel*, must of its nature have, as it were, a veto over the temporal. The arguments which justified Pius VI in condemning the Civil Constitutions of the Clergy, or Pius XI in condemning the *Action Française*, are the arguments which justified St. Pius V in deposing Elizabeth.

Such decisions, it is true, are not infallible. The declaration of moral principle is infallible; the judgment on fact is fallible. A pope might be deceived concerning what the sovereign had done. A wicked pope might even use his prestige to pervert the facts and thus harm an enemy for some purely secular reason. The Catholic who was honestly convinced, and could prove, that the Pope was either deceived or in bad faith would be excused from obedience to such a decision. Yet for all that, it is the sort of decision which, in extreme cases, the Pope has a right and a duty to make, the Catholic a right to demand from his Pope.

Nor was there anything new or outrageous in the Pope's command to Catholic Europe to enforce his decision. The doctrine that a revolting province could be brought back into the Catholic unity by force was the doctrine which had saved us in Spain, at Murêt, where Simon de Montford broke the Albigensians, and at half-a-dozen other times. We to-day live in a European society which owes its survival to the preservation of its religious unity for fifteen hundred years and which could not possibly have survived had not force sometimes been used to preserve that unity. It is very easy for us, enjoying the benefits which our ancestors preserved for us, to sit back and condemn the barbarity of the means which they used for thus preserving those benefits. There has never existed a civil society which has not claimed the right in the last resort to protect itself by force. We are apt to refuse that right to the Church because the modern decadence has taught us to think of Her not as a single society, but as a mere collection of isolated souls. But She is more than a collection of some hundreds of millions of God's children. She is the single bride of Christ. She exists not primarily for the benefit of man, but for the greater glory of God, and, once we understand that She is a society, we cannot deny that Her right to preserve Herself is far more unquestionable than that of any civil society can ever be.

It may be objected that the forcible re-establishment of Catholicism would have been followed by persecu-

F

tion. There is little doubt that this is true and little doubt that that persecution would have been accompanied by all those vilenesses with which religious persecution has always been accompanied (it makes little odds to the accompanying vilenesses, whether the faith that is persecuting be false or true). Yet the persecuted would have perished, and the persecutors would soon afterwards have perished, too, but Catholic England would have survived. Both sixteenth century Catholics and sixteenth century Protestants are to be blamed for their cruelty, but it is no argument against the return of justice to say that in an age in which both just and unjust governments preserved their power by cruelty, if justice had returned, it would have returned hand in hand with cruelty. Truth is great and must prevail—even against the sins and blunders of its supporters.

CHAPTER IV

MARY AND ST. BARTHOLOMEW

ST. PIUS' Bull and the suppression of the Rising of the North left Elizabeth and Cecil faced with two difficult and connected problems. What should they do with Mary? What should be their policy towards the Catholics?

As long as Mary was alive her name would provide a cause for which the discontented in England and the Queen's enemies on the Continent would inevitably plot and fight. Cecil, therefore, whose way in these matters was the simple way, was for killing. So, too, on the Scotch side, was "yours to command, John Knox, with his one foot in the grave." Elizabeth had scruples. Mary was a sovereign and the killing of a sovereign, even if another sovereign was the killer, might prove itself a most unpleasantly effective hint to those who had their grievances against the conditions of the times. Besides, Mary, whatever crimes she may or may not have committed in Scotland, had certainly committed none since her imprisonment in England. She had thrown herself on Elizabeth's protection in answer to Elizabeth's own invitation. She had been most scrupulous to lay before Elizabeth the Duke of Norfolk's proposal of marriage, and no evidence could bring home to her any responsibility for the Northern Rising. She had been privy to it, but she had opposed it. The cold-blooded murder of the helpless suppliant would have been a crime that might shock, Elizabeth feared, the consciences even of sixteenth-century courtiers. To such gentlemen there was still a divinity that hedged a queen, even when they saw very little sanctity in the life of the subject. There was a risk that the blunder of such a crime might bring nearer that Franco-Spanish alliance for which the Pope was now so desperately working.

Elizabeth probably guessed that it was unlikely, if she herself should live much longer, that she would be able to resist the growing pressure upon her and preserve Mary's life. But at least she was determined that she should not be saddled with the responsibility for her death. "Can I put to death the bird that, to escape the pursuit of the hawk, has fled to my feet for protection?" she said. "Honour and conscience forbid." "No human power," she told the Scotch ambassador, "will ever persuade me to sign the warrant for Mary's execution." She therefore proposed to return Mary to Murray, the Scotch regent, on condition that he would promise to kill her. The plan would not do for Cecil, who wanted Elizabeth herself saddled with the responsibility.

Spain was the old ally of England and it did not at first seem likely that Elizabeth's accession would break the alliance. So little did Philip at the beginning intend to carry out St. Pius' sentence against Elizabeth, that, when the Bull was issued, he assured her that nothing that the Pope had ever done had so greatly displeased him. He did not wish the Bull to be enforced, and was only anxious that, if it were enforced, he himself should receive the vacant throne of England. Yet as time went on, commercial rivalry with England reminded him of his Catholic duty. Though he was always personally devout, yet it was only under pressure that he allowed piety to dictate his politics. But now more and more he became inclined to make Mary's cause his own, and there grew up a dangerous off-chance that a mismanagement of the problem would play into the Pope's hands and allow him to create the Catholic League for which he was working. It was therefore important that England should draw closer to France.

The French court, which hated Spain a great deal more than it loved Rome, was willing enough, and negotiations were opened for a marriage between Elizabeth and the French King's brother, the Duc d'Anjou. King Philip at once sent his agents to arouse English Protestant feeling against the marriage by the argument that the Protestant settlement would be in danger if the Queen was married to a Catholic husband. Though the truth was the opposite and by the marriage the chances of a Catholic restoration would have been wholly destroyed, yet the argument was not ineffective.

The negotiations for the marriage broke down because of the Duke's demand for formal permission to practise his religion. Yet they led to the signature of a treaty of alliance between Elizabeth and Charles IX of France. According to that treaty, Elizabeth had wished the French to promise that they would defend her in the event of an invasion of England, "though the invasion be made on account of religion." They did, it is true, object to such very plain speaking, but, to show how little they cared for St. Pius' Bull, they were willing to substitute the phrase, "in all cases of invasion whatever."

Mary is sometimes spoken of as if she was a wanton fomenter of discord against Elizabeth's Government. But surely, if we consider the dishonour of the Government's conduct to her, we must admit that it is rather remarkable that she should have so long continued to look hopefully to her cousin for justice. But now at last, guessing that the main purpose of the French treaty was to enable Cecil to kill her with impunity, she began to intrigue by means of Ridolfi with Philip of Spain, her one source of hope. The marriage between the Duke of Norfolk and Mary was made part of a Catholic plot. Mary was to be declared Queen, and the King of Spain was asked to invade the country on her behalf. Ridolfi claimed to have promises of support from forty English peers. The claim was almost certainly false, and the Duke of Alva, to whom Ridolfi first went, advised his sovereign against having anything to do with the business. A more practical plan was, he said, to marry Mary, not to the Duke of Norfolk, but to Don John of Austria, Philip's half-brother, the victor of Lepanto. St. Pius V, on the other hand, expressed his good-will towards Ridolfi's scheme and gave some money, but said that its practicability depended upon Philip's willingness to take it up. Ridolfi came to the court of Madrid, filled with tales of hopes and promises and plots that were plainly exaggerated, if not wholly false. Philip's own inclinations seem to have been to agree with Alva and have nothing to do with the plan, but, in response to St. Pius' plea that the honour of Catholic Christendom could not allow Mary to be killed without a blow being struck, he half-heartedly agreed to co-operate. He was perhaps led to his preference for Ridolfi's plan over Alva's by his jealousy of his half-brother, Don John.

The knowledge of the plot came to Cosimo de Medici, the Grand Duke of Florence, a friend of the French, the enemy of Spain and a distant cousin of Catherine de'Medici, the French Queen-mother. He at once betrayed it to Elizabeth. A spy, called Baily, was arrested and incriminating letters were taken on him. Norfolk, though he stoutly asserted his innocence of the treason, was seized and executed; Mary still lived on.

The story only convinced Elizabeth that her safety demanded that she make a second pretence of allying herself by marriage with the French court. If Anjou would not have her, what, she suggested, about his brother, Alençon? Alençon's main disadvantage was that he had two noses; his main advantage that he was an atheist, and would, it was thought, declare himself Protestant, or anything else, if it could be shown to be worth his while. He was of the stuff of which many persecutors were made. For a time he had turned Huguenot and then, when political convenience dictated a reconversion to Catholicism, he had attempted to prove his sincerity by presiding at the destruction of a Huguenot town. The Flemings had made about him the rhyme:

Flamands, ne soyez étonnés,
Si à François voyez deux nez,
Car par droit, raison et usage,
Faut deux nez à double visage.

It seems to have been as just as it was witty.

Negotiations were opened between the two courts and were proceeding smoothly, when suddenly the whole French situation was very violently changed. The policy of the French monarchy had been to hold the balance between the two great parties of France—the Catholic party under the Ducs de Guise and the Protestant under Coligny and the House of Navarre. Such a policy of professed impartiality often means in practice the favouring of the weaker party. So it was in France in these times. The nation had refused the Reformation; yet its national policy, both at home and abroad, was Protestant. Coligny sat at the king's right hand. Catherine de' Medici, a skilled judge of such situations, saw that an intensely Catholic public opinion would not much longer tolerate such a policy.

To the student of the English sixteenth century it may seem a strange language which speaks as if there were such a thing as public opinion. Yet a vocal, active, French public opinion was not first created by the Revolution. Even at this date, public opinion, which in England was a phrase without meaning, was in France a reality. In spite of the slackness and cynicism of politicians it refused to allow France to be robbed of the Catholic faith. By its presence Catholicism was saved. The Huguenots were unpopular at the best times. The peasant and the Parisian shop-keeper laid at their doors the responsibility for the horrors and the disturbance of the civil wars, and they had goaded people to fury by their massacre of Catholics in Southern France on St. Bartholomew's Day, 1569. Catherine saw that the party of the Guises would before long launch their attack upon the Huguenots. It would succeed, and, if that attack should find the monarchy still in alliance with the Huguenots, then monarchy and Huguenots would go down together.

She therefore determined to reverse the royal policy while there was yet time and to free the monarchy from its fatal alliance. In the politics of sixteenth-century France there was apt to be but one weapon with which to rid oneself of either friend or enemy— the weapon of the assassin's knife. On 22nd August, Catherine caused an attempt to be made upon the life of Coligny. It failed, and Coligny was only wounded. The Huguenots showed by their language that they looked upon this attempt as a declaration of war. To prevent such a war, on St. Bartholomew's Day of 1572, the anniversary of the Huguenot massacre, Catherine de' Medici and Charles IX let loose the mob of Paris upon the hated Huguenots. The madness spread from Paris to the provinces, and then, as is usual, savage massacre begat savage counter-massacre wherever the Huguenots were in strength. Sir Walter Raleigh, who happened to be in France during these days, speaks in his *History of the World* of how he watched the Catholics being smoked out of the caves in which they had taken refuge in the Languedoc hills.

The part played by Catherine and Charles was purely cynical and calculating. But to the Parisian Catholic the Huguenot was a man who was trying to rob him against honour of his most treasured possession. He dealt with his enemy in one of those tremendous out-bursts of explosive energy to which the French resort every now and again against those who would rob them of a precious right. St. Bartholomew was a bloody business. Yet it was less bloody than war, and, had the Huguenots not been driven from power by violence, whether by the violence of war or of massacre, they would have remained masters of the French state. Henry IV would not have declared himself Catholic, and, had a central Protestant monarchy been established in France similar to that which was established in England, our civilisation could hardly have survived. France must have been drilled out of Catholicism as England was drilled out of it. The Thirty Years' War must have ended in a complete Protestant victory, and Catholicism have been forced back within the boundaries of the Alps and the Pyrenees.

Yet for all that, the bloody reprisal is to be con-demned, for the individual has no right to take upon himself the responsibility for ordering the deaths of others. Nevertheless, it is only fair to the French to admit that the moral standards of political life at that time were at such a level that neither Elizabeth nor any of her contemporaries were deeply shocked by it. They did not shrink from the French monarchy as from a tainted thing. They were concerned only to see how the changed situation affected themselves. To Elizabeth the news of St. Bartholomew was bad news.

Cecil persuaded her that the Alençon marriage, though the project of it was later to be revived, was for the moment out of the question, that the Anglo-French alliance was of very doubtful strength, and that a Franco-Spanish alliance had become dangerously possible. The new situation could only turn to Elizabeth's advantage, if it should be discovered that Catherine de' Medici, by forestalling the Guises, had stolen their thunder. If that should prove to be so, then the Franco-Spanish alliance would not have been brought nearer, but would have been banished to a more distant future. Yet it did not look as if this improvement was at all likely to last, nor did it last. Elizabeth, interpreting the situation aright, wisely treated St. Bartholomew as a setback. She acted in characteristic fashion. She professed at first to be shocked, but afterwards to be perfectly satisfied at the explanation of the little incident which Charles IX's ambassador offered. At the same time, Cecil dispatched aid to the remnant of Huguenots who were in arms at La Rochelle. In order to frighten the French a flimsy Anglo-Spanish alliance was patched up.

Yet the main lesson which Cecil professed that Elizabeth should learn from her dangers was that there was no time to be lost in the killing of Mary—"that devilish woman," as Walsingham called her. He proposed a plan similar to Elizabeth's own old plan. The Scotch were to be got to do the killing, and Killigrew was sent as Elizabeth's agent to arrange with Marr, the new Scottish regent, about the conditions. Marr made several stipulations, of which the most important was that Elizabeth should pay the debts which he owed to his Scottish soldiers. If this were done, he promised that Mary would not live for four hours after she came into his hands. Yet, to make sure that he and his friends were not in any way suborned, Cecil insisted that Elizabeth should hold their children as hostages until the deed was done. It was a pleasant bit of work and might have been carried through, had not Marr himself died four days later, probably of poison.

CHAPTER V

THE OPEN WAR

So much for the moment for Mary and the foreign problem. It is necessary to turn back to Elizabeth's relations with the English Catholics. If one looked at Europe as a whole, it was by now becoming daily clearer that neither was the full Catholic unity going to be reimposed upon the Continent nor was Catholicism going to be wholly destroyed. On the one hand, the Roman unity was permanently broken and the boundaries of Europe's new divisions beginning to show themselves. On the other hand, under the growing influence of the Jesuits, Catholicism had recovered from its first inertia and, so far as the religious problems were to be settled by debate, was now winning its debates all along the line.

From the first, Cecil, as I have said, had had but one object—to decatholicize England. From 1558 to 1570 or so, he was occupied in accustoming people to the new ways, and during these years it was important, if it could be managed, to prevent an open papal offensive. He succeeded. He was now able to meet offensive with offensive, and there began the second period—the period of frank persecution.

He determined to make more strict the conditions

of religious conformity. In the first years of Elizabeth's reign, Catholics had widely practised the custom
which was known as "reconcilement"—a custom by
which people used to go first to the Protestant Church,
then hurry off and confess their fault to a priest and
hear his Mass. As Saunders says:

"Atque ita vel vi vel arte factum est ut maxima
catholicorum pars, usque adeo his primis initiis non
perspecto rei periculo, hostibus paulatim cederet,
ut schismaticorum ecclesias, conciones, communio-
nem ac conventicula, aliquando publice adire non
recusarent. Ita tamen ut interim missas secreto domi
per eosdem saepe presbyteros, qui adulteria hereticorum sacra in templis publice peragebant, aliquando per alios non ita schismate contaminatos,
celebrari curarent; saepeque et mensae Domini ac
calicis daemoniorum, hoc est, sacrosanctae Eu-
charisticae et Calivinicae, uno eodemque die, illo
luctuoso tempore participes fierent. Imo quod magis
mirum ac miserum erat, sacerdos nonnunquam,
prius rem sacram domi faciens, deferebat pro catho-
licis, quos ipse id desiderare cognoverat, hostias
secundum formam ab ecclesia usitatam consecratas,
quas eodem tempore iisdem dispensabat, quo panes,
hereticorum ritu confectos, caeteris, Catholicae
fidei minus studiosis distribuebat."*

Such conduct was justified by a variety of more or
less specious arguments. Some excused attendance
at Matins and Evensong with the plea that these

*My attention was called to this passage by my friend, M. Pierre
Janelle, of Strasbourg.

services were little more than the Offices of the Bre-
viary, translated into English; others explained that
their attendance was limited to mere bodily presence
and that they took no part in the service. For such
conduct priests very freely gave absolution. Indeed,
they could hardly refuse it, when, as we have seen, so
many of them were themselves officiating in one way
or another at both services, and the priest must presumably have very often had to say his Mass without
even receiving absolution from another priest for his
celebration of the Anglican service. Nor indeed, even
if he did receive absolution, can the absolution have
been of any value, since it would clearly not be pre-
ceded by any firm purpose of amendment. Mary
Stuart reports to Gregory XIII as late as 1575 that
Catholic gentlemen in her household, thinking that
they can serve her better if they conceal their religion,
regularly receive the Anglican Communion and afterwards get absolution for doing so from her chaplain.

The tolerance of this strange custom was obviously
largely due to a wish not to add unduly to the difficulties of the faithful. There was more to it than that.
In the temper of the sixteenth century no political
movement could succeed unless it had men of wealth
to lead it. Even such a man as St. Ignatius, for instance,
—who had no illusion at all concerning the moral
superiority of gentle over common folk—yet saw that
under the conditions of his day it was important to
attract gentlemen into his company. Taking the snob-
bish world as he found it, he saw that a cause which
desired to succeed must first find gentlemen to lead
it. Now, owing to the bribe of the abbey lands, the

Catholics were especially weak in men of wealth. The poor were willing to follow, but they had no leaders. If the wealthy Catholic had refused to attend the Anglican service, the Government would have been given an excuse to reduce him to poverty. It was thought best for the cause that by outward conformity the rich should, as far as possible, keep their riches. The Spaniards had even asked that permission for "reconcilement" should be officially given by the Papacy, but, impossible as such a request was and ultimately indefensible as was the custom itself, yet the line of argument by which it was defended is easily intelligible. The practice was as offensive to Cecil as it was to the Pope, and Cecil now determined to prevent it. Reconcilement was declared high treason. The Queen had previously only persecuted people for not being Anglicans; she now began to persecute them for being Catholics. By the laws of 1571 Cecil finally abandoned his pretence that he persecuted only for conduct and not for opinion.

It may seem strange that England suffered herself to be robbed of her religion so tamely. It *is* strange, nor is there any denying that the Elizabethan English, physically brave, were yet, on the whole, a morally feeble and servile lot. As Mr. Hubert Hall concludes from his exhaustive studies of the Elizabethan state papers, "the state of society was the worst that had ever before been in the land." Yet the feebleness of the resistance is partly to be explained, I am sure, by Cecil's cleverness in exempting both peers and also the Marian bishops from the penal statutes and the oath of supremacy. This exemption, for which it would be hard to think of any defence in justice, meant that those who would naturally have led the resistance to tyranny succumbed, unless they were of an heroic temper, to the temptation to be content that they themselves could hear Mass in their own houses and evaded the dangerous duty of popular leadership.

In Cecil's first period of rule bloody persecution of Catholics had been for the most part a threat; during the second, it was a fact. Elizabeth tried to bluster and to escape responsibility. "My bishops are a set of knaves and I will not have the Catholics misused," she said, and it is, I daresay, true that if she could have had her way things would have been much milder. She could not have her way.

The causes of the changed policy were partly the Rising of the North, the problem of Mary Stuart, the Papal Bull and Cecil's growing security. There was soon added another and perhaps an even more important reason for persecution. At first Cecil had been content to remain undisturbed by the activities of the non-juring Catholic priests—"Queen Mary's priests," as they were called. They were not allowed to preach. Only those of the clergy who had received a special licence and who could be relied upon to use their opportunity to denounce "the Pope and all his superstitious usurpations" were allowed to preach. The rest could only read very dull homilies on very minute points of controversy. Doubtless, like the Puritans later, many neglected the prohibition. Yet even so, Cecil was satisfied that "Queen Mary's priests" would all in time die out and that there would be an end of the trouble. So it would have been, had not a certain

G

Lancashire priest, one William Allen, founded in 1568 an English seminary at Douai for the training of priests for the English mission field. It was this recruitment of the Douai college and of another College which was founded at Rome in 1579, which taught Cecil that Catholicism would not naturally die out in England. It must be eradicated.

In the policies of the Catholic princes during these years there is little that can move us to admiration. The story is a sordid story. Very different is the tale that we find when we come to the missionary priests, those glorious men, the heroes of Elizabethan Catholicism. Panegyric is quite beyond the purpose of this book, yet the reader cannot understand this period unless he understands the nature of these men, the men against whom Cecil waged his war. They cannot be described better than in the quotation of a couple of pages from a Protestant historian, the great German, Meyer.

"More intimate knowledge of the mission priests teaches us to regard them as men of strong, manly character, steadfast in their belief and unruffled in their obedience—men whose self-control seldom failed them and whose cheerfulness was seldom disturbed, who were transfigured by their victory over the world and filled with love for all men without distinction—men finally who, amidst the most terrible torments and ill treatment, remained free and unconquered because to them martyrdom was the crown of life. 'Our vocation is not to be inclosed in cells,' wrote the Jesuit, Robert Southwell, in his

Meditations, 'far from intercourse with men, but to combat openly, and, while rebuking the irregular devices of others, we must be watchful that we are not overcome by our own. Among the loquacious observe moderation of speech, among the irascible guard the temper, among the lovers of pleasure beware of self-indulgence . . . for the least blot in a religious is a great deformity.' The man who wrote these words lived up to them. The cruelties of Topcliffe make our blood boil even at the present day, but Southwell, who had been tortured ten times, had no harder word for him than 'Thou art a bad man.' To accept calmly the most insulting speeches and to answer without bitterness was a point of honour with every priest, especially the Jesuits—their schooling at the seminary stood the test when tried by this fiery ordeal.

"The powers of whole classes of men, as of individuals, increase with the greatness of the task set before them. In no other European country at the time of the Counter-Reformation did the Catholic Church possess clergy who discharged their priestly duties with such a holy zeal as the little band that worked in England. 'The souls of Catholics are more precious than our bodies,' might stand as the motto for the history of the mission. The reproach of secularity usually brought against the clergy would not have had any justification in Elizabethan England. Not even the most prejudiced opponent could discover anything to find fault with in this respect. It was the heroic period of the mission. Heroism was the offspring of persecution. When the humane Charles I put a stop to the persecution and took the Catholics, both clerical and lay, under his protection, they ceased to be heroes and saints and once more became men subject to human frailties. The only fault that can be found with the priests of the Elizabethan age is that their contempt for death often took the form of contempt for life and yearning for martyrdom. No worldling ever showed greater eagerness in the pursuit of worldly honour than they did in pursuing the 'crown' and the 'palm.' Their chief fear was that God would think them unworthy of this honour, and in speaking of their brethren's martyrdoms their words often ring with impatience to be following in their steps, and frequently it sounds as if they were even envious of their lot. When at last the hour of their passion was at hand they gave gifts to the jailer as he put their feet in irons, or expressed their gratitude to him in words, if they had nothing else to give. To the curses heaped upon them by the people on the way to prison or to execution they responded by blessings, and beneath the gallows they kissed the hangman's hand, reddened with the blood of martyrs. We may admire this or think it mistaken or fantastic, but at any rate these men were giving a practical turn to the precept, 'Bless them that curse you.'

"The same deeply religious spirit which reminds us of the early days of Christianity is to be found too in the preface to the Catholic translation of the Bible, the greatest literary achievement of the Rheims seminary. 'So we repine not in tribulation but ever love them that hate us, pitying their case and rejoicing in our own. For neither can we see during this life how much good they do us; nor know how many of them shall be (as we heartily desire they all may be) saved: our Lord and Saviour having paid the same price by His death for them and for us. Love all, therefore, pray for all.' In this estimate of their vocation there was no difference between Jesuit and secular. The first years of the Jesuit mission which fell within the period when this heroic spirit was at its height show not only an equal eagerness for self-sacrifice in all, but also the heartiest co-operation between Douai and Rome. The division that had already arisen in the college in Rome did not at once spread to England. 'Here, forsooth, we have so many enemies in common that there is no time for internal factions.' "

Just as Cecil's policy towards the Catholics may be roughly divided into periods, so, too, may the Catholic policy towards Cecil. Throughout the 1560's Catholic resistance to the Elizabethan settlement was so chaotic and so unorganised that it can hardly be said that there was a Catholic policy at all. Allen first gave to Catholicism a policy of resistance, and organised and thought-out resistance begins with St. Pius' Bull and the appearance in England of the first seminary priests about 1570. The period of resistance may be divided again into two—a period of non-political resistance which lasts until experience, and in particular the death of Campion, shows it to be ridiculous, and a period of political resistance. The first policy both of the seminary priests and of the Jesuits, who in 1580 associated themselves with this work, was frankly to recognise that England had ceased to be a Catholic country in the official sense of the phrase, to ask for only that part of a Catholic life which was of absolutely divine command—the Sacraments—and to refrain from all politics. They came to England with express instructions from the General to confine themselves to apostolic work and to the administration of the Sacraments. These instructions were obeyed. The Jesuits are often blamed because in Elizabethan England they mixed religion with politics. The truth is rather that the Jesuits were the first people to make an entirely honest attempt to do a thing which no Elizabethan had ever before attempted to do—to divorce politics from religion. The Campion case was of the first importance. For it convinced Persons, Campion's friend, that in a foreign invasion was the only possible hope of saving the Mass for England. The Jesuits did not wantonly attack Elizabeth; it was more nearly Elizabeth who wantonly attacked the Jesuits.

Let us take one example of how Cecil treated the non-political seminary priest and one example of how he treated the non-political Jesuit.

The first of the seminary priests to fall into Elizabeth's hands was one Cuthbert Mayne. The story of his trial is important in any consideration of the charge that Catholics in Elizabeth's reign were only executed as traitors. Controversialists sometimes write as if they had only to prove that Catholics were executed for treason and they had then proved that there was no such thing as religious persecution. Such argument escapes the point. The Mass is the centre of Catholic life. The Elizabethan Government forbade the Mass. Therefore it persecuted for religion. Some will have it that the Catholics were very unpleasant people, that they were traitors, that there were plots for the assassination of Elizabeth, that the Mass is a ridiculous piece of mumbo-jumbo, that people are better without it, and the rest. Such arguments might prove that religious persecution was justified. They could not possibly prove that there was not any religious persecution.

An absolute despotism can make up whatever law it likes. If it chooses to count drunk anyone who has consumed a single glass of beer, then a man who has consumed a single glass of beer is legally drunk. The Elizabethan Government chose to say that to bring an *Agnus Dei* into the country was a crime. Whoever brought an *Agnus Dei* into the country was then legally a criminal. But to pretend that the word under such circumstances carries with it any moral connotation is an intellectual dishonesty.

You could not get a better example of this manufactured treason than that which is given by the trial of Mayne. Mayne had been harboured by a certain wealthy landowner, named Tregian. Tregian was an ex-courtier who is said, on contemporary evidence, to have incurred Elizabeth's displeasure by resisting her improper advances. Likely enough as such a tale is, a more certain motive for the attack on him is that his lands were coveted by the Queen's cousin, Sir George Carey. The excuse that he had harboured Mayne was therefore taken, and both Mayne and Tregian were apprehended.

The case against Mayne gives an instructive lesson on the nature of Elizabethan treason. Mayne was indicted and executed for treason. The charges against him were (1) that he had obtained from the Pope a "faculty" containing absolution of the Queen's subjects; (2) that he had published this at Golden; (3) that he had taught the ecclesiastical authority of the Pope to prisoners confined with him in Launceston Goal; (4) that he had brought into the realm an *Agnus Dei* and given the same to Mr. Tregian; (5) that he had said Mass. Yet people are content to teach in the schools that the Catholics were executed as traitors and leave to the unread student the impression that "treason" under Elizabeth meant what it had meant in the days of her predecessors or what it means to-day.

Mayne's trial had a further importance in the development of the Cecilian law. Though the chief charge against Mayne, the charge that he had said Mass, was certainly true, it was not possible to prove it. The jury were therefore instructed that against notorious Catholics proof of treason was not necessary. "Strong presumption" was sufficient to justify a conviction. The jury objected to this new doctrine and the fiery sheriff of Cornwall, one Richard Grenville, the godfather of Kingsley's Amyas Leigh, had to force his way into the jury-room and bully them into bringing in the required verdict, on the strength of which Mayne was "hanged, cut down still living, then ripped up, disembowelled, beheaded and quartered." For his "good service" Richard Grenville was knighted. He had, as students of Lord Tennyson will recollect, "only done his duty as a man is bound to do," but this particular incident in his career is somehow or other omitted from Charles Kingsley's *Westward Ho*.

It is customary to argue that we must not condemn those who inflicted savage penalties because the age was one of savage penalties. It is true that generation differs largely from generation in its estimate of the exact degree of severity which seems to it to fit the crime. What appears harsh to one appears humane to another. Yet through all the changes man preserves always his sense of justice, and our complaint is not that such men as Mayne were savagely punished for their crime, but that they were savagely punished for no crime at all. Grenville must have known that no crime had been committed. Caring only to win the favour of the powerful and of the Government and thus to assist himself in his social climb, he compelled the jury to bring in their unjust verdict, and it is folly, not charity, which tries to excuse the wickedness of Grenville and of the masters of the terror.

Alongside of that of Mayne put the story of another and a better known man, Edmund Campion. Edmund Campion was one of the noblest and most lovable, one of the most honest and most English of all Englishmen, "one of the diamonds of England," as Cecil himself admitted. Born in the important year of 1540, the year in which the destruction of the monasteries gave to the new masters of England that vast economic motive for the decatholicizing of their country, he had found himself in the early years of Elizabeth's reign at Oxford, where he was Fellow of St. John's College. It is a sign of the confusion of minds in those first years, before the Pope had given any clear con-

demnation of the Elizabethan changes, that even such
a man as Campion should have been willing to receive
deacon's orders in the new Church of England. Yet
he soon repented of this, resigned his orders, was
reconciled to the Church of Rome and fled, first to
Dublin and afterwards to the Continent. He joined the
Society of Jesus and was sent to work in Bohemia.
When it was decided that the Society should be associated with the mission to England, Campion and
Persons were chosen to be the leaders of the work.

"The Reformation," writes Johnson in his preface
to *Macbeth*, "did not immediately arrive at its meridian
and, though day was gradually increasing upon us,
the goblins of witchcraft still continued to hover in the
twilight." The metaphor is the opposite of the truth.
Such men as Cecil and James I, mumbling at their
demonologies, were not men who had not yet freed
themselves from past shackles. They were rather men
who, having revolted from the free service of faith,
had been captured instead by the bondage of superstition. The contempt and astonishment of such a
free, Catholic mind as that of d'Espes, the Spanish
ambassador, at the superstition of the atheist English
is instructive proof of this.

Never was this superstition more rampantly seen
than at the first coming of the Jesuits. At the time of
the election of St. Pius V it was said that "a comet,
like blood, stood over London and near its tail a hand
issued from a cloud and brandished a sword." So now
the Jesuits' coming was accompanied by the whole
conventional catalogue and paraphernalia of marvels.
There was "an earthquake in London which made the

great bell of Westminster toll of itself and threw down
great portions of the Temple Church and of Christ
Church, Newgate Street, at sermon time, and slew
two persons; in June great storms of thunder and hail."
A vision of a hostile fleet was seen off the sea at Bodmin,
a pack of hounds seen and heard in the air in Wilt-
shire; in Somerset three companies of men in black
each sixty strong, marched through the sky. More
surprising still, "one Alice Perrin, eighty years of age,
brought forth a monster with a head like a helmet, a
face like a man, a mouth like a mouse, a human body,
eight legs all different, and a tail half a yard long."
Another lady "gave birth to a monster that was male
and female with mouth and eyes like a lion." Those in
our day who have from time to time the privilege of
entertaining the genial fathers of Farm Street may
congratulate themselves that the comings and goings
of their guests are no longer accompanied by such
extremely embarrassing gynæcological eccentricities.

According to the rules of the Society of Jesus it is
forbidden for its members to take part in quarrels
between Christian princes. The Jesuits therefore only
accepted their task on the express condition that the
work required of them should be purely apostolic.
They obtained from the Pope the decision that "*rebus
sic stantibus*," the Bull of Deposition was not binding
upon English Catholics.

It is true that the Papacy was playing a double
game and that, at the same time that it was sending
Campion and Persons into England to release Englishmen from the Bull, it was sending Nicholas Saunders and
a papal army into Ireland in order to put the Bull into

execution in that country. Yet there was no parallel between England and Ireland, for England was an independent country, but Ireland, so ran the papal argument, a papal fief which the Pope had granted to the Kings of England, but which he had freely granted and could freely take away again. Henry VIII had usurped the royal title over Ireland. The Kings of England before his day had been only Lords, not Kings, of Ireland. They held it in trust and not of right.

Whatever be the weight of that argument, it was certainly an argument for which the Jesuits were not at all responsible. The knowledge of the Irish expedition, when Campion and Persons came to learn of it only a little before they themselves sailed for England, made no difference to their honest obedience to the instructions which they had received. "If any of you can prove me guilty of any crime except my religion, I will willingly agree to suffer the extremest torments you can inflict," Campion challenged his accusers. In spite of that rigid obedience, the sincerity of which no serious writer has ever attempted to disprove, the Government made it their first business to lay hands on Persons and Campion. Persons escaped them, but owing to the assistance of an informer they were able to arrest Campion at Lyford Grange, in Berkshire, on 16th July, 1581.

The Government might have contented itself with saying that there was war to the death between the Elizabethan State and the Catholic Church, that Campion's ideal of a Catholic England, frequenting the Mass and at the same time loyally obedient to the

Queen and the sacrilegious party using her name, was an ideal apart from reality, and that therefore whoever received a convert made an enemy to the Queen. Such was doubtless their belief; there was some truth in it, and it would have been an honest argument. Yet public opinion cannot be wholly neglected. There was a limit to what even the Elizabethans would stand from their masters. The object of Cecil was to de-catholicize England, but even in 1581 he did not dare openly to declare his object. Campion was therefore forced to stand a joint trial with six others and there was trumped up against him a fantastic tale of a plot, concocted at Rheims against the Government. For his complicity in that plot Campion was to die. Of the pretended conspirators some, it was proved, had never in their lives been at Rheims, others had never met until they found themselves standing side by side in the dock. The Government shamelessly rammed into the indictment the names of any priests whom it happened to have in custody and for the killing of whom it was unable to find any other cause. No writer, Catholic or non-Catholic, has ever pretended that the evidence upon which Campion was condemned was anything but a fabrication of lies or that either the prosecution or the packed jury did not entirely know it to be so. Hallam writes that "the prosecution was as unfairly conducted as any perhaps that can be found in our books." "The most unjust verdict," said an old writer, "that ever, I think, was given up in this land, whereat already not only England but all the Christian world doth wonder and which our posterity shall lament and be ashamed at." According to Camden,

Elizabeth herself was in no doubt of Campion's innocence.

> You bloody jury, Lee and all the eleven,
> Take heed your verdict which was given in haste
> Do not exclude you from the joys of Heaven,

ran a popular metrical commentary on the trial.

The Duc d'Alençon, who was at that time in England negotiating for Elizabeth's hand, was the only person who might perhaps have saved Campion. Elizabeth would have found it difficult to refuse his intercession. A deputation therefore went to interview Alençon and to beg his assistance in saving a co-religionist's life. The Duke's confessor ushered them into the presence of His Grace. They found him waiting to begin a game of tennis. He listened courteously to what they had to say and when they had finished stood for a time stroking his chin with his left hand. Then he raised the racket in his right hand as a signal to his opponent. "Play," he shouted. The game commenced and Campion's hope of life was gone.

When the jury came back into Westminster Hall, bringing with them their verdict of guilty, Chief Justice Wray, before passing his sentence, turning to Campion, asked, "Campion and the rest, what can you say why you should not die?"

Campion replied in a speech of which the last sentences were as follows:

> "The only thing that we have now to say is that, if our religion do make us traitors, then we are worthy to be condemned, but otherwise are and have been

as true subjects as ever the Queen had. In condemning us you condemn all your own ancestors, all
the ancient priests, bishops and kings—all that was
once the glory of England, the island of saints and
the most devoted child of the see of Peter. For what
have we taught, however you may qualify it with
the odious name of treason, that they did not uni-
formly teach? To be condemned with these old
lights not of England only but of the world by their
degenerate descendants is both gladness and glory
to us. God lives; posterity will live; their judgment
is not so liable to corruption as that of those who are
now going to torture us to death."

Campion ceased; and the voice of the Chief Justice
was heard, passing upon the prisoners the sentence of
hanging, drawing and quartering. "*Te Deum lauda-
mus*," sang Campion. "*Haec est dies quam fecit Dominus;
exultemus et laetemur in illa*," cried out Sherwin, one of
his companions.

"Sir," said Dr. Johnson of poor old Dodd, "when a
man knows he is to be hanged in a fortnight, it con-
centrates his mind wonderfully." These words of
Campion I have quoted not because they are fine
rhetoric, though indeed they are rhetoric as fine as
any that even Westminster Hall has ever listened to,
but because of their truth. In them is the issue, seen
clearly, stated clearly, separated from irrelevancies
and unanswerable.

Many Catholics during these difficult days were
guilty of follies of one sort or another which gave to
Cecil excuses for what he did. There is no denying it.

But if the follies of these Catholics be pleaded in justification for Campion's death, we can but answer with Cardinal Allen, "If Pius V addressed Nicholas Morton sixteen years since about the matter of excommunication in England, shall all priests and Jesuits be deemed traitors therefore? If Dr. Saunders, either upon his own zeal and opinion of the justice of the quarrel, or at the Pope's appointment, were in the wars of Ireland employed for the defence of the Catholic religion against the Protestants, may you by your laws or any other Divine or human ordinance condemn therefore to death a number that never knew either the man or the matter? Some pretence may you have to be offended with the Pope, and perhaps lack no laws to punish the said two Doctors, that never were either of the Society or seminaries, but to make guilty all priests and Catholics, at home or in banishment, is too unreasonable, and to murder so cruelly one man for another's fault is too foul and intolerable iniquity." Nor does the folly or crime of these Catholics alter the issue, that issue which it is vital that we should not allow anyone to mis-state.

People speak loosely, as if there had been in England something of the nature of a modern, secular, liberal state, as if this state had in the past lived, off and on, in a kind of alliance with the Papacy and that alliance it was in the sixteenth century thought expedient to renounce. Such talk is nonsense. It is as if one spoke of a leg getting tired of belonging to one body and electing to transfer itself to somebody else. The Church had made England. England was a limb of the body of Christendom. Cut off that limb, and you cut

England off from the whole of her past. To Catholics that past was a past founded upon divine things. But even the historian who refuses the Faith cannot deny the fact. Froude, the great enemy of Catholicism, has contrasted the Catholic and the Elizabethan hierarchies in a paragraph of fine-cut and splendid prose, which stands out before us like a mountain.

"A Catholic bishop holds his office by a tenure untouched by the accidents of time. Dynasties may change—nations may lose their liberties—the firm fabric of society may be swept away in the torrent of revolution—the Catholic prelate remains at his post; when he dies, another takes his place; and when the waters sink again into their beds, the quiet figure is seen standing where it stood before—the person perhaps changed, the thing itself rooted like a rock on the adamantine basements of the world. The Anglican hierarchy, far unlike its rival, was a child of convulsion and compromise: it drew its life from Elizabeth's throne and, had Elizabeth fallen, it would have crumbled into sand. The Church of England was as a limb lopped off from the Catholic trunk; it was cut away from the stream by which its vascular system had been fed; and the life of it, as an independent and corporate existence, was gone for ever. But it had been taken up and grafted upon the State. If not what it had been, it could retain the form of what it had been—the form which made it respectable without the power which made it dangerous. The image in its outward aspect could be made to correspond with the parent tree."

H

To create such an unreal and outward correspondence was the purpose of Cecil and his party, as Froude's great but unscrupulous mind so clearly saw. Yet they did not dare to proclaim their purpose quite openly. It would have seemed to the Elizabethan Englishman a thing unthinkable that England should cease to be a member of the Christian unity. The change had therefore to be concealed behind talk of a reform of abuses, of abolition of corruptions, of a preservation of the essentials. It was such talk that was exposed in its nakedness in Campion's great rhetoric, when he laid bare before his countrymen the very nature of that evil revolution of the rich.

In 1580 an ill-judged papal expedition landed in the south-west of Ireland. That aggression, the success of the Douai seminary and the offensive of the Jesuits, were made in 1581 the excuse for new and yet more stringent penal laws. "A sort of hypocrites, Jesuits and vagrant friars have come into the realm to stir sedition," complained the Queen. They must be dealt with. The details of the new laws make tedious reading, nor can the student have much curiosity to learn exactly what new treasons the Crown lawyers found to lurk in the practice of Catholicism. It is beyond the purpose of this essay to go into statistical controversies concerning the numbers who suffered under these statutes or into details of the methods which the Government employed to collect their evidence, into debates upon torture or gaol-fever, into an examinatory interpretation of what exactly Cecil meant by his disarming phrase, "all manner of gentle ways of persuasion used." The cause of religion will not be at all served if we discuss the defeats of the Church in the temper in which people discussed German atrocities during the war. Of the general effect of this policy upon the country a word must be said.

One of the many good reasons why it is undesirable to resort to religious persecution if it can possibly be avoided, is that, however pure may be the cause in whose name the persecution is to be carried out, it is very difficult to preserve the purity of the persecutors' motives. The persecutors are themselves weak and fallible beings. The blackmailer and the informer and the *agent provocateur* are certain to make their unpleasant appearance. The underlings are tempted to gain the favour of their masters by the vigour of their persecution, and, where they cannot find those who are really guilty, are always tempted to manufacture evidence against the innocent. The masters of the persecution, having at the first argued in their fanaticism that the guilty must be extirpated, easily slip from that into the argument that the terror of the governed is necessary to the security of the Government. Such familiar symptoms the Elizabethan persecution showed. Take, for instance, Walsingham's warning letter to Sir Henry Sidney, President of Wales, telling him that not nearly enough Catholics have been apprehended in his district for the Queen's liking and that "his doings were narrowly observed."

Then again there is the continual temptation to the persecutor to use his power to remove from his path some person whom he makes out to be a religious offender, but who is really merely the persecutor's private enemy or one whose goods he covets. Of persecution from this motive it is not hard to find examples in the Elizabethan times, whenever the persecutor was strong enough to make himself master of the condemned's property. Elizabeth's own phrase was that the penal laws should be enforced "for profit and gain's sake." To cite every example of their enforcement from such a motive would be to tell the whole history of the sixteenth century.

The chief persecutor of the Catholics was a certain Richard Topcliffe. He first took to his trade after the Northern Rebellion through his anxiety to get hold of the lands of one Richard Norton, of Norton Conyers, in Yorkshire. Soon afterwards we find him quarrelling with Sir Christopher Wray, the Chief Justice who afterwards condemned Blessed Edmund Campion to death, over the appropriation of a prebendal stall in Lichfield Cathedral. The evidence for his atrocities comes not from his enemies or victims but from his own boasts. "Because the often exercise of the rack in the Tower was so odious and so much spoken of by the people, Topcliffe had authority to torment priests in his own house in such sort as he shall think good," and he himself boasted that, in comparison with his private machine, the official racks were mere child's play. After his torturing of Robert Southwell public opinion was so disgusted that Cecil had to pretend to arrest him for having exceeded his powers. It was but a pretence and he was soon out and at work again. In 1594 he brought against one Fitzherbert an action which throws a curious light upon the state of public morality among the governing class at that time. Topcliffe sued Fitzherbert for five thousand pounds, on the ground that Fitzherbert had promised to pay him that sum if he would get Fitzherbert's father and uncle and a certain Mr. Bassett condemned for recusancy and then torture them to death. Both sides admitted the contract. Topcliffe maintained that he had fulfilled the conditions; Fitzherbert denied it. Mr. Bassett, he said, was still alive, and, though the father and uncle had, it is true, been tortured and were now dead, yet it could not be proved that torture was the cause of death. Fitzherbert maintained that they had died from gaol-fever. Even the Elizabethan court felt that there were some limits beyond which baseness should not be publicly advertised and "the matter was put over for secret hearing." Yet nine years later we find that Topcliffe has somehow managed to annex the estate of the Fitzherberts to his other possessions.

One other story in illustration must suffice. There was a certain gentleman of Warwickshire, a Mr. Arden, a cousin of some sort, it seems, of Shakespeare. He had been so foolhardy as to refuse to sell some land which he possessed to Elizabeth's favourite, the Earl of Leicester. Arden had a son-in-law called Somerville, a Catholic and a lunatic. In one of his fits of insanity Somerville asserted, or was said to have asserted, that he would murder all Protestants and the Queen at the head of them. On this excuse Arden was arrested, though he had, it seems, had nothing to do with his son-in-law's eccentricities. With Arden was arrested Hall, a missionary priest, whom Arden had kept in his house disguised as a gardener. Both Arden and Hall were put to the torture, and on the rack Hall was induced to admit that he had once heard Arden express a wish that the Queen was in Heaven. On this evidence Arden was convicted of a conspiracy to kill the Queen and executed, and his lands were seized by Leicester. An authority as little opposed to the powers that be as Camden wrote: "The woeful end of this gentleman . . . was generally imputed to Leicester's malice. Certain it is that he had incurred Leicester's heavy displeasure, and not without cause, for he had rashly opposed him in all he could, reproaching him as an adulterer and defaming him as a new upstart."

There was then about the Elizabethan persecution every one of those features by which every persecution is necessarily made so very unpleasant. Blackmail and espionage were rife to an almost incredible degree, and, employed at first for the purpose of the persecution, soon spread, as is their custom, into every department of life, until Cecil, the Queen's Secretary of State, dare not write to Lord Shrewsbury, of the Queen's Council, because he knows that spies will seize the letter and take it to the Queen. "A father," reports the Spanish ambassador, "dares not trust his own son." To be a spy became an international profession. Scoundrels, taking the money both of Elizabeth and Philip, sold the secrets of each to the other and invented secrets where they were not able to discover them.

Yet the Elizabethan persecution had about it also an additional unpleasantness from which most religious persecutions have been free. Lord Arundel, the Elizabethan courtier, was convinced of the truth of the Catholic faith by watching the trial of Campion and by listening to the staged debates between him and his Anglican adversaries. He became a convert and was therefore arrested for treason. He wrote before his arrest to complain that the people who surrounded the Queen were atheists at heart. Leicester, it seems, was almost confessedly atheist. Walsingham, the patron of the free-thinking Marlowe, was suspected of being so, though the language of Protestantism was always ready to his tongue. Elizabeth and Cecil had been Catholics yesterday and would be Catholics again to-morrow if it should be found necessary in order to save their skins. In Mary's reign, when the burnings were on, Cecil had made himself quite ridiculous by going about everywhere with a rosary, mumbling away at his prayers, and to show his zeal he had crossed over to Brussels in order to escort Cardinal Pole to England. He was now, of course, as vigorous in his outward professions of Protestantism, but, if he believed in anything, it was probably in magic and witchcraft.

Sir Walter Raleigh, too, though he was not at that time of the Council, was widely believed to be atheist and this reputation clung to him right up to the time of his calamitous but well deserved death, which Archbishop Abbot, though he admitted that Raleigh died "a religious and Christian death," yet ascribed to insolence brought on by his "questioning" of "God's being and omnipotence." At this date in "Sir Walter Raleigh's School of Atheism," according to *An Advertisement Written to a Secretary of my Lord Treasurers of England by an English Intelligencer*, "much diligence was said to be used to get young gentlemen to this school, wherein both Moses and our Saviour, the Old and the New Testaments, are jested at and the scholars taught among other things to spell God backwards."

For the predominance of atheism in Elizabethan society evidence comes from writers varying as widely in
opinion and motive as Thomas Nashe at one end and
Robert Persons at the other. It is to the honour of the
Church of England that very few of those who persecuted in her name believed in her tenets. As Cardinal
Allen wrote with the bitterness of an *émigré*, but yet with
much truth, the contest is "not for religion of which our
enemies have not a bit, but for the stability of the
empire and worldly prosperity."

In modern times the controversy about the Elizabethan persecution is sometimes carried on in very
peculiar terms. One side is apt to complain that all
the Catholics were traitors, the other side loudly to
protest that but a disreputable minority had anything
to do with treason. As if they were a sort of Labour
Members who obediently paid their income tax though
Cecil and the Conservatives happened to be in power!
It is impossible to make head or tail of the story if you
speak as if treason or loyalty to Elizabeth meant the
same thing as treason or loyalty to George V, or use
the word "traitor" as a mere term of abuse. It is
always to the interest of those in power to give the
word an ugly sound. Yet, as Elizabeth's own god-son,
John Harrington, wrote,

Treason doth never prosper. What's the reason?
That, if it prosper, none dare call it treason.

The parallel is not with the government of George V,
but with such governments as those of Lenin or Calles.
A queen with a claim more than doubtful at the first—
a perjured queen, who only received her throne on

the express condition that she would maintain the Catholic religion and had broken that promise—a queen who was a puppet in the hands of those whose policy was the destruction of English life—such was the Elizabeth to whom English Catholics were asked to be loyal. As for her masters, they were rich men and it is not for us to judge them. As Anatole France has said, "*La miséricorde de Dieu est infinie; il sauvera même un riche.*"

It is true that even during the later years of Elizabeth's reign there were many loyal Catholics. In spite of the papal Bull, the Catholics, in the petition presented by Richard Shelley in 1585, protested their loyalty and reminded Elizabeth of the important theological truth that even the Pope cannot justly command what is sinful. The Armada was to arouse no Catholic revolt. Yet Catholic loyalty was a loyalty of despair, and there is no doubt that from the death of Campion and the time of the adoption of the official aggressive policy up to the defeat of the Armada— that middle period during which the Government was tyrannous and not yet national—an enormous proportion of the Catholics, though perhaps willing to bear in submission so long as there was no hope of remedy, would yet have declared against Elizabeth if there had appeared to be a reasonable hope of overturning her.

People are too apt to think of Elizabethan England as they find it depicted in such books as Charles Kingsley's *Westward Ho*. It is necessary to banish from the mind all this talk of Gloriana and the birth of England, of Elizabeth as if she were a sixteenth-century Queen Victoria, only slightly less German, and the ludicrous pretence that no one ever thought of intriguing with a foreigner until the wicked Jesuits put them up to it in the days of good Queen Bess. The error is to transfer to these earlier years that romantic feeling for the old queen which the later Spanish menace created and which lasted until it was drowned beneath the great unpopularity which she earned from the execution of Essex. Kingsley's Elizabethans walk through the English streets, conscious that they live at the dawn of a new era of freedom and adventure, that they have broken with the old and shackled past. "We owe the great writers of the golden age of our literature," Shelley tells us in the Introduction to *Prometheus Unbound*, "to that fervid awakening of the public mind which shook to dust the oldest and most oppressive form of the Christian religion." If it be so, the Elizabethans themselves seem to have been quite unaware of it. We search the real Elizabethan literature in vain for a trace that the Elizabethans had any such feelings about themselves. Rather did they feel—and they were quite right—that they lived in an evil and violent time. They did not especially look forward to the future; rather did many of them, like Shakespeare, look back with a regret, perhaps a merely sentimental regret, to good old times before the universal scramble, to the life of status and to

> The constant service of the antique world,
> When service sweats for duty, not for meed.

As Carlyle said, Shakespeare's poetry is "the last sunset glory of the Middle Ages."

To what would you have had a Catholic be loyal in this second period of Queen Elizabeth's reign? Governments, it is true, have certain rights simply because they are *de facto* governments. When we recollect that the much quoted line

There's such divinity doth hedge a king,

was put into the mouth of Hamlet's uncle, the usurping regicide, who made such a very bloody beginning and was to come to an equally bloody end, we may suspect that the sixteenth-century monarch-worship was perhaps mixed with a slightly larger dose of quizzical irony than is sometimes understood. Nevertheless, the age certainly did possess this peculiar vice which was strong to reinforce the legitimate respect for authority. Yet, unless you would have the subject the slave of an Oriental despot, the duty of obedience, as has been already said, is not absolute. A Catholic lived in those days under perpetual sentence of death. At any moment of the night or day he knew that his house might be suddenly broken into and he himself carried off to prison and perhaps to death. If he owned any property, he was at the mercy of any neighbour who wished to delate him. False priests, hirelings of Walsingham and Cecil, had come to him, heard his confession and then betrayed its secrets to the Government. He had perhaps been called to the rack and there tortured for no offence of his own, but simply to induce him to say something that would incriminate a friend or a co-religionist. Nicholas Saunders writes:

"Sometimes when we were sitting merrily at table,

conversing familiarly on matters of faith and devotion (for our talk is generally of such things), there comes a hurried knock at the door, that of a pursuivant. All start up and listen like deer when they hear the huntsman; we leave our food and commend ourselves to God in a brief ejaculation; nor is word or sound heard till the servants come to say what the matter is. If it is nothing we laugh at our fright."

Even if such a Catholic fled abroad, the spies of the Government would follow him, watch his movements, and, if he were a person of importance like Cardinal Allen, perhaps even attempt to remove him by poison or assassination.

For a time the Catholic had perhaps thought it wise to tolerate this reign of terror because it could not last for ever and after it saner times would return with the accession of the Queen's cousin. He now saw that there was little doubt that, in order to prevent the return of those saner times, somehow or other, sooner or later, the Queen's cousin was going to be done to death. The murder of Campion had shown that a Catholic could not save his life by merely keeping out of politics. Is it to be seriously argued that the Catholic who saw a chance of delivery from such a tyranny should refuse that chance simply because the deliverer happened to be a foreigner? As Maurice Clennock wrote with obvious sense, "Better to attain eternal blessedness under a foreign lord than to be cast into the nethermost hell by an enemy at home." You might as well have told the Patriarch Tikhon that he had a duty of loyalty to Lenin because Lenin happened to be living in the Kremlin. The wonder is not that there was so much, but that there was so little Catholic disloyalty. Nor is it remarkable if some considered the use of what was at that day the common weapon of Scotch and French politics, the assassin's knife.

It is most important that this question should not be discussed in the terms of modern Liberalism. The importance of the point must excuse a repetition. To the Catholic the first and most essential concern is that he should be able to get the Sacraments. Yet the life of the Church is more than the isolated lives of the individuals who make it up, and the Catholic can only live his full life in a Catholic community; for his religion does not stop at the church-door; it infects every activity of life. It is right that English Catholics to-day should recognise that they live in a non-Catholic community and they are foolish if they waste too much time in complaining at the necessary disadvantages which such a life imposes upon them. At what exact date it became proper for the Catholic to admit that England was no longer a Catholic country and so to adjust his policy is debatable. He could hardly be blamed for refusing to recognise it in the early years of Elizabeth's reign. The Elizabethan Catholic, living in the first years of the Counter-Reformation when in every country but England the new Protestantism was losing all along the line, could not have been expected thus complacently to sit down to England's loss to the Faith.

"For men to kill each other about a piece of bread appears, when so stated, the supreme culmination of human folly," writes Froude. Precisely; but, as he goes on to admit, when so stated the problem is stated as falsely as it possibly could be. Neither on the one side nor on the other was it thought that the issue was simply whether Tom and Dick and Harry should have Mass. The issue was whether England should or should not continue to be a Catholic country. No man could have been more loyal to Elizabeth than Blessed Edmund Campion. His loyalty was quite extravagant, and of all the perversions of justice of those times there was none more shameless than that by which he was done to death. Yet there was a certain shrewdness in his persecutors. The Jesuit ambition, though honourable, was apart from reality. The Jesuits had got the Pope to agree that *"rebus sic stantibus"* Catholics were not under obligation to obey the Bull. But the loyalty which only agrees not to rebel so long as rebellion is hopeless is a dangerous and qualified loyalty. The papal policy in Ireland, where the Vatican was open in its support of rebellion, showed very clearly what the papal policy in England would be, if only an opportunity could be found. And, Bull or no Bull, no power on earth could have persuaded Catholics to tolerate permanently the supremacy of Cecil and his party. Cecil knew very well that an England which was taught to demand the Mass would be an England which, whatever its leaders might advise, would yet certainly demand a radical change in the country's property system and would not for long tolerate the rule of those whose power was founded merely upon successful sacrilege. For the Catholic there is a temporal as well as a spiritual obligation. But it is a very muddled confusion which thinks that, for that reason, the Church either has, or ought to have, nothing to say upon temporal or political problems. There is a Catholic social order and such an order a Catholic population will inevitably demand from its rulers. Cecil was determined to decatholicize England and he rightly saw that England could only be decatholicized by persecution.

The teachings of Luther, on the other hand, had included a defence of the rights of the landed classes that was almost lunatic in its violence. In his pamphlet *Against the Murderous Robbers Hordes of Peasants*, he had written: "It was not only princes and magistrates who should make an end of them. Every honest man had the right to be judge and executioner of such scoundrels and to slay them as one would kill a mad dog." In his sermons he had spoken of the desirability of slavery. "There was good scripture warrant for it. . . It was the lack of strong government that created discontent among the rabble and the workers." Erasmus had accused the Lutherans of being "men with but two objects at heart, women and money." And to Cecil and the Elizabethans, while to commit oneself to such a theology would be perhaps a trifle narrow-minded, it was at least most important to "comprehend" it.

Luther, the man of straw, played into the hands of the enemies of all religion. Up to this time all but a small minority in England still shrank both from the violence and from the lucidity of Calvin. The issue was still left between Paganism and the Church. That issue was whether Catholic freedom should survive or whether there should be established the dominance of the Pagan State, omnipotent alike over the conduct and over the consciences of men.

CHAPTER VI

THE DEATH OF MARY

WE must turn once more to the story of Mary. The death of Marr for the moment saved Mary's life. Yet to Cecil's mind there was no time to be lost. The Tudors were an unhealthy family and there was always the fear that Elizabeth might die on his hands and leave Mary alive and unquestionable Queen of England. There was the fear, too, that Elizabeth's death might be hastened by assassination.

Cecil and Walsingham had filled Elizabeth with stories of plots in order to frighten her into action. How far these plots were genuine and how far they were manufactured it is to-day hard to discover. Certainly there was, as we shall see when we come to the Babington plot, much forgery and falsehood, but at the same time there was no great motive in manufacturing the evidence of plots except to awake in Elizabeth a realisation of a danger which did exist—and certainly the danger did exist. There were plots, even if not always exactly the plots which Walsingham professed to have discovered, and the fates of Orange, Coligny and Murray showed very adequately how insecure was the life of a sixteenth-century Protestant leader.

Of the tales of mere atrocities, whether piled up by

the one side or the other, it is sufficient to say this. There was a state of war between Catholicism and the English state. It was one of those fundamental wars in which both sides felt that, if they lost, everything was lost. In such wars each side will use every weapon upon which it can lay its hands. We to-day are fortunate to live in a society whose morals do not countenance assassination, nor does the whole form of our society stand or fall with the survival or death of one man or woman, as did the absolute monarchies of the sixteenth century. Our problems are wholly different. Yet it is by no means impossible for an honest man to argue that a code of morals, which permits war in the last resort when diplomacy is not sufficient, should logically permit tyrannicide when war is not sufficient. Shakespeare—to take the instance of a man of the sixteenth century who stood outside its political controversies—thought that it was wrong for Macbeth to murder Duncan because the cause was unjust, but he did not doubt at all that it was right for Hamlet to murder his uncle, where the cause was just, though merely a cause of just revenge. Perplexed by every other doubt, Hamlet never doubts of his duty to kill.

> Is't not perfect conscience
> To quit him with this arm? and is't not to be
>   damn'd
> To let this canker of our nature come
> In further evil?

Such was the feeling of the sixteenth century.

A few men, such as John Knox, "applied to his fellow-Christians," to quote Andrew Lang, "the com-

I

mands which Israel supposed to be divinely directed
against foreign worshippers of Chemosh and Moloch."
The death of the enemy was pleasing to the Lord and
he viewed it, to quote Mr. Edwin Muir, his latest
biographer, with "a delighted contemplation." In
such an attitude there was a spice of lunacy, but the
common opinion was perfectly sane. Most men assassi-
nated opponents exactly as Englishmen killed Germans
in the war. It was a regrettable necessity but a necessity, and both Catholics and Protestants used this
weapon against their enemies. Catholics massacred on
St. Bartholomew's night and in the Netherlands.
Huguenots covered all South-West France with their
barbarities and Englishmen shot down Irishmen as if
they were wild beasts.

Protestants succeeded in assassinating Cardinal
Beaton—"the godly act of James Melvine," John Knox
called it—and tried to assassinate Cardinal Allen.
Catholics succeeded in assassinating the Prince of
Orange and tried to assassinate Elizabeth. "Since
that guilty woman of England," wrote the Cardinal of
Como, Gregory XIII's secretary and confidant, "rules
over two such noble kingdoms of Christendom and is
the cause of so much injury to the Catholic faith and
loss of so many million souls, there is no doubt that
whosoever sends her out of the world with the pious
intention of doing God service, not only does not sin
but gains merit, especially having regard to the sentence pronounced against her by Pius V of holy
memory. And so, if those English nobles decide actually
to undertake so glorious a work, Your Lordship can
assure them that they do not commit any sin."

At the first it seemed likely that Mary would save her enemies the trouble of killing her by herself dying of the effects of her imprisonment. This would have been most convenient. Unfortunately for Elizabeth she recovered. There was, thought her friends, but one person who could perhaps save her life—her son, James VI. If Mary died he then became Elizabeth's heir and, if only James could be induced to declare himself a supporter of Mary's policies and Mary induced to resign to him her rights, as she would then be very willing to do, there would be hardly any gain in killing her.

The chances of the chaos, which was the Scotch politics of that day, aided by skilful French intrigue, had in 1581 freed the young James from the captivity of the Regents and restored the Scotch monarchy to a certain independence. Lennox, Mary's friend, was for the moment powerful at James' court, and James needed money. He therefore pretended to fall in with the schemes of Mary's supporters. He professed his friendship to the Catholic cause and in consequence was able to obtain a subsidy from Philip of Spain.

In August of 1582, after what is known as the Raid of Ruthven, James was once more a prisoner and Lennox had to flee the country. "God had stirred up a faction of the nobility against the Government," reported Calderwood. It was, to tell the truth, the sort of thing that God seemed to be somewhat fond of doing in sixteenth-century Scotland. Yet, in spite of it, in the next year the King got free again and Elizabeth appeared to be faced with a real possibility of a Franco-Spanish-Scotch alliance for the liberation of Mary. To avoid the danger, she was willing to capitulate and accepted the French king's offer of his ambassador, Castelnau, as an impartial chairman to arrange the conditions of Mary's release.

Yet on the one hand the Spaniards had no mind to have Mary saved by the French alone. "Nothing," wrote Mendoza, the Spanish ambassador, "could be more injurious to Spanish interests and to the hope of converting the island than that the French should get their fingers in through the Queen of Scots and turn things to their own ends!" On the other hand Henry III, while professing his support of Mary's cause, never intended to see Elizabeth's quarrels with the Scotch settled. If they were, she would then, as he knew, be free to give more effectual aid to the Huguenots. He therefore secretly instructed Castelnau to see that the negotiations failed, and once more Mary's hopes were dashed to the ground.

Yet even now she might have been saved had she not been the victim of a piece of baseness more horrible by far than that of Henry III. Pathetically enough, Mary, disillusioned of all the rest of the human race, had yet kept till now her faith in the honour of her own son. James had professed his devotion to her cause and had received from Philip the price of devotion. He had sent one Gray to Paris to arrange the plans for Mary's liberation. This Gray he now dispatched as ambassador to Elizabeth with instructions to sell those plans to her for a further price. Gray did so; Mary's last hope was extinguished and James received his price.

From Gray Elizabeth learnt—what she had already learnt from Throckmorton and from some papers which the Dutch had captured from the Jesuit, Creighton—that the Duc de Guise was preparing to invade England on Mary's behalf. A plot there certainly was, though preparations for it cannot have gone very far, since even Stafford, Elizabeth's ambassador in Paris, had to confess that he found no signs of preparations for its execution. Yet for the first time James' treachery had put into Elizabeth's hands some evidence by which she could really raise among the religiously indifferent a cry of "*la patrie en danger*." For the first time Elizabeth's cause began to appear to some as a national cause. Those to whose financial interest it was to preserve the Elizabethan settlement could not allow Elizabeth to be killed. An association was started of persons who bound themselves to defend the Queen and to punish all who should attack her. Everybody naturally joined—both those who wished to assassinate Elizabeth and the rest. It was like joining the Fascists in Italy or the Ku Klux Klan at the height of its power in a southern state of the U.S.A. Nobody was willing to face the risks of not belonging. Mary herself asked to be allowed to join.

Cecil took advantage of the popular feeling to push through the Parliament of 1584 still further penal and confiscatory Acts against the Catholics. Parry, a spy of Cecil, had been engaged in Paris in some doubtful intrigues with Mary's undependable confidant, the factious Morgan. As a reward he had been put into Parliament for Queenborough. Perhaps considering himself to have been insufficiently rewarded, he was now anxious to expose his master and he denounced the new laws "as a measure . . . pregnant with fines and forfeitures which go to enrich not the Queen but private individuals." He paid on the scaffold the usual penalty of truth. He was executed in 1585 for complicity in those "treasons" of Morgan's, for the stirring up of which, as an *agent provocateur*, he had in 1584 been personally rewarded by Elizabeth. Orders were given for services of thanksgiving for the Queen's escape from danger to be said in all churches.

An Act was also passed by which, in the event of a rebellion, not only the rebels but the persons also in whose name the rebellion was raised should suffer the penalty of high treason. It only remained to arrange the rebellion.

There was little real danger of an invasion by the Duc de Guise. France was in no condition to launch out on a Quixotic adventure. But Spain, alone of the great powers of Europe, was untroubled by religious divisions. The tradition of Spanish friendship for England died hard—that tradition which Cardinal Granvelle expressed in the phrase "Spain must defend London as it would Brussels." Spain could ill afford to quarrel with a country that lay right across the communications between the mother country and her richest province. But now, at long last and too late, Spain was beginning to wake up to her religious obligations. If the Spanish danger was to be avoided, it was necessary for Elizabeth skilfully to exploit Spanish difficulties in the Netherlands. One result of the reaction against Protestant influence in the French government had been to deprive the revolting Dutch of French help. The Dutch, in desperate state, therefore turned to their only other possible deliverer—to Elizabeth. They begged to be allowed to become her subjects. The full admission of their request would have dealt to the system of Europe and to the rights of sovereigns a blow more violent than Elizabeth could afford. Yet, though she refused to admit them as subjects, Cecil compelled her to admit them as allies, and Leicester and an army were sent to their assistance.

Mary was now in a sad way. Even her friends, instead of devising some last and desperate plan for her salvation, were wasting their time in mutual recriminations concerning the responsibility for past failure. The disastrous quarrel between the Jesuits and the seculars was at its height. Morgan and Paget, Mary's French agents, bitterly complained of the Jesuits, who had been responsible for the introduction into the plot of the traitor, Gray. A very efficient system of espionage and blackmail, organised by Elizabeth's secretary, Walsingham, kept a watch upon every letter and every person who approached Mary. She had previously had the right to communicate direct with Mauvissière, the new French ambassador, and thus to send letters to Elizabeth which did not pass through Walsingham's hands. Walsingham and his friends did not trust Elizabeth and thought, rightly enough from their point of view, that she was too friendly to Mary. Walsingham, therefore, now determined to close, and succeeded in closing, this channel. The men who were the masters of this system had convinced themselves that the death of Mary was necessary to their own safety, and there was now little doubt that evidence upon which Mary could be put to death would be discovered before long.

Walsingham is often held up to us as the type of Elizabethan Protestant statesman. Yet, be that as it

may, there was never a man who acted more unvary-
ingly upon the motto which slander ascribes to the
Jesuits that "The end justifies the means." His means,
considered simply by themselves, no code of morals
could justify. Yet there was in him a dignity which
many of the Elizabethan courtiers lacked. He cared
for more than money; he was the servant of an idea.
It is common to say that the cause to which he devoted
his life was the cause of Protestant freedom. What is
stated positively should, I fancy, be stated negatively.
The motive for all his action was not love of Protestantism but hatred of Catholicism. To the destruction of
Catholic truth he bent the whole energy of his great and
tortuous mind, much as a Lenin bent all his energies
to the destruction of capitalist Europe. For the achievement of the purpose of the one as of the other all means
were legitimate.

Into the tangled question of what was true and what
was false in the conspiracy that is known as the Babington plot it is not possible to enter. The story of it—its
spies, its pretended conspirators who were really
government agents, its tampering with letters and the
rest—reads more like pages from a novel by William le
Queux or Baroness Orczy than a sober chapter in
English history. The facts, so far as they are necessary
for our purpose, were these. Whether or not the suggestions of a conspiracy came from an *agent provocateur* of
Walsingham, called Gifford, or whether the originator
was a foolish but honest plotting priest called Ballard,
it is impossible to decide. Yet a conspiracy there
certainly was, and, if you care to call it so, a Catholic
conspiracy. Its object was to assassinate Elizabeth, to

rescue Mary from Charteley, where she was then im-
imprisoned, and to set her upon the throne. It was
hoped that the Duke of Parma would send over a
Spanish army from the Netherlands. There was certainly an inner ring of conspirators, to which Babington
belonged, who were determined to carry out the full
programme. As certainly the conspiracy had much
wider ramifications, and the greater number of the
conspirators were only aware of the purpose of freeing
Mary and knew nothing of the plan for the assassination of Elizabeth.

The English have, it seems, an especial talent for
espionage. The English government's secret service
has, from the time of Elizabeth to our own day, always
been greatly superior to that of any other power.
So now the conspirators were as children in Walsingham's hands. Their plans were known to him from the
first. They were given sufficient rope to hang themselves—and, what was more important, to hang Mary—
and were then seized, and, of course, executed. Elizabeth specially requested that the death of the conspirators should be "protracted to the extremity of
pain," and with the first victims this was done, but the
horror of the crowd at the barbarity of the execution
compelled the executioners to dispatch the remainder
more quickly. Their lands were, as usual, distributed
among the courtiers, Sir Walter Raleigh receiving a
large slice of Babington's. Walsingham, who had hoped
to get this slice for himself, went into the country to
sulk immediately after the execution of Mary.

On the charge of complicity in this plot Mary herself
lost her life. That Mary was involved in the plot, so

far as it was a plot for her liberation, is not denied. She herself admitted it very freely. What she did deny was that she had been privy to any project for the murder of Elizabeth. In spite of Elizabeth's effort to tempt her into confession by a promise of pardon she persisted in this denial to the end.

Impartial public opinion of the day did not greatly blame her, even when it supposed her guilty. According to the conventional moral standards of sixteenth-century courts, people had often felt themselves justified in resorting to assassination in order to remedy grievances much smaller than those which Mary had suffered at the hands of Elizabeth. *"Etant née princesse souveraine et détenue prisonnière par si long temps contre raison,"* reflects Châteauneuf, who had by now succeeded Mauvissière as French ambassador, *"elle ne peut être blâmée, quand bien elle auroit fait tout ce dont elle la veult charger, si elle a cherché tous les moyens de se déliverer."* Yet we are concerned not with a problem of casuistry but of history.

The claim of the Government was that there were letters written by Mary's secretary, Curle, to Babington at the Queen's command, in which the project of Elizabeth's assassination was discussed and approved. Mary maintained that if the letters contained any such discussions, then the discussions had been inserted without her knowledge. Such was the accusation and the answer to it. In order to form a judgment of the truth it is necessary to make the acquaintance of a certain Gilbert Gifford.

Gilbert Gifford was the scapegrace son of a respectable Catholic father. Being in need of funds, he had early sold himself to Walsingham as an *agent provocateur*. After other adventures at the English College at Rome, from which he was eventually expelled, he had made his way to the seminary at Rheims, where he got himself ordained priest and there persuaded a certain John Savage, a priest of small intelligence, that it was his duty to go to England to assassinate Elizabeth. That accomplished, Gifford then made his way to Paris, where he soon insinuated himself into the confidence of the foolish Morgan, then a prisoner in the Bastille.

I have already explained how Walsingham had succeeded in closing the channel by which Mary Stuart was able to hold direct communication with Châteauneuf, the French ambassador, and thus to send letters to Elizabeth and to her friends which did not pass through Walsingham's hands. It was important that she should have such a channel, and Gifford persuaded Morgan that he would be able to manage secretly for Châteauneuf what Walsingham would no longer allow him to do openly. Therefore, as Châteauneuf records:

"In the month of December, 1585, Gifford came to England with letters from the Archbishop of Glasgow, Morgan and Paget, which testified to his Catholicity and fidelity to the Queen of Scotland. . . . The French ambassador had then appointed Cordaillot, one of his secretaries, to attend to the affairs of that Queen, and he, on seeing Gifford's letters, asked him the reason of his journey. Gifford said that he had been entrusted with secret letters for the Queen of Scotland and that as she was now confined in a house not far from his father's home he hoped to be able to accomplish the task. Cordaillot nevertheless answered little, for he knew that Walsingham was endeavouring to find out whether he corresponded secretly with the Queen. . . . He was not yet trusted and eventually withdrew. It was afterwards discovered that he was lodging with Phelippes, a servant of Walsingham."

Yet it was essential to Châteauneuf and to Mary that a channel of communication should be found, and it was not long before Gifford was able to persuade the unwary Châteauneuf that he was able to "deliver the goods." A plan was arranged by which Mary should give her letters to a certain brewer of Burton whose duty it was to deliver beer at Charteley every week. Mary thought that the brewer smuggled the letters out of the castle in the inside of his beer casks and then delivered them to Gifford and that they were handed on by Gifford to those to whom they were addressed. The truth was more complicated. These letters "the honest man," as the brewer was always called in Walsingham's correspondence, handed at once to Paulet, Mary's gaoler. By him they were sent to Walsingham, by whom they were opened, transcribed and read. Phelippes, Walsingham's decipherer, was an expert forger and, if it should seem desirable, he could always be employed to alter the letters by interpolations or added postscripts. According to Camden, in the important correspondence with Babington which brought Mary to the scaffold, he certainly added the request for the names of the six men who were going to

assassinate Elizabeth and perhaps made other addi-
tions as well. *"Quibus subdole additum eodem charactere
postscriptum, ut nomina sex noblilium ederet, si non alia."*
After being read by Walsingham and tampered with
by Phelippes, the letters were given back to "the
honest man," who then delivered them, as if they had
come fresh from Mary, to Gilbert Gifford, whom "the
honest man" believed to be a sincere servant of Mary.
Gifford then forwarded them on to their destinations
or sent them back to Walsingham according to his own
discretion. "The honest man" was meanwhile making
the most of his important opportunity by charging
Paulet an outrageous price for his beer.

It is certain that Mary's letters were sometimes
falsified in this way. That being so, it is, to say the
least, possible that she was telling the truth when she
said that the particular letters in which she was made
to refer to the project of assassination were falsified.
What motive, on the one hand, could Mary have had
for thus giving herself away ? However anxious she
was for Elizabeth's assassination, was it likely that she
would have been such a fool as to express her approval
in writing ? On the other hand, the whole object of
Walsingham's policy was to secure evidence which
would convict Mary, before the world, of conspiracy.
What more likely than that Walsingham should have
inserted these discussions of assassination ?

There is, as Lingard has pointed out, an argument
of internal evidence to support the probability of
forgery. Mary is made to say at the beginning of her
letter that "upon the accomplishing of this design I
may be so suddenly transported out of this place."

Later she warns her friends against moving before they have made adequate preparations since "it were sufficient excuse given to that queen, in catching me again, to enclose me in some hold out of which I should never escape." Now "the design," according to the argument of the Government, meant the assassination of Elizabeth. The difficulty in that argument is clear. According to it Mary was not to be rescued from Charteley until "the accomplishing of their design," until, that is, Elizabeth was already killed. Whatever problems the future might hold for Mary and her friends, that of a recapture by Elizabeth could then hardly be one, since Elizabeth would by that time be already dead.

So conscious was Walsingham of this weakness in his case that he instructed Serjeant Puckering, the counsel for the prosecution, to argue that Mary meant to give instructions that no attempt should be made to rescue her "before either they had a strong army in readiness to place her in or they had dispatched Her Majesty." Yet the words of the letter, as it emerged from the hands of Phelippes and Walsingham, could not possibly bear this meaning. Is it not more probable that Phelippes had blundered and, inserting the one passage, had failed to notice the discrepancy between it and the other?

Nor, even if we suppose that Walsingham did not falsify Curle's letters, was there any proof that Mary was privy to all their contents. Had he been able to do so, Walsingham had an easy opportunity to prove his case. When first Babington offered his services to Mary, Mary wrote a minute of the answer to be sent. This minute the first secretary, Nau, expanded into a letter in French which Curle then translated into English. Either Walsingham had seen this original minute or he had not. If he had not seen it, he was in no position to say that the copy was a faithful copy. If he had seen it, then he was under obligation either to produce it or at the least to explain what had become of it. He professed that he possessed both Mary's minute and Nau's letter, but, when challenged to produce them, was unable or unwilling to do so. Asked for Mary's minute, he contented himself with "wishing to God that it might be found."

It was pretended that there was a minute of Nau's which had clearly been the source from which the letter found in Babington's possession was composed. Yet, when this minute was produced, it was found to be nothing of the sort. It consisted of a lot of jotted French notes, which ended *"De Flandres en même—Ecosse au même temps—Coup—Sortie."* *"Coup"* it was pretended, must refer to a blow of assassination at Elizabeth. The argument was puerile.

A large fuss was made because Babington on the scaffold had admitted that the letters of Mary which he received contained references to Elizabeth's assassination. What of it? Babington had certainly received in good faith what he imagined to be Mary's letters. The question was whether they were Mary's letters or whether they had been tampered with by Walsingham.

An attempt, too, was made by threats of the rack and by confusion of the issue to trap the two secretaries into condemning their mistress. Nau, called before the council on the day after the Babington conspirators had been executed with the most ruthless barbarity, seems in his terror to have behaved in a somewhat tortuous way. Yet substantially the attempt to wring any valuable admission out of them failed. It was pretended to Mary that they had made confessions, but her judges refused her demand to be confronted with them, and long after those terrible times were passed— in 1605—Nau bore witness that the main charge against Mary had been *"fausse, calomnieuse et supposée."* He challenged any of those who then examined him to deny that he had maintained so at the time.

It is sometimes argued that this doubtful question has been for ever settled by Teulet's publication in his *Relations Politiques* of a letter written on 10th September, 1586, by Mendoza, then Spanish ambassador in Paris, to Philip II. Mendoza there writes: "The Queen of Scotland, as it seems to me, must have known the affair well from that which one reads in a letter she has sent me." Mendoza was an intelligent man whose business it was to be well informed. At first sight the evidence of this sentence would seem to be conclusive. Yet, as Teulet said, "To decide the question one should have the letter." In 1885 Dr. Bernard Sepp, in his *Der Rücklass der Maria Stuart*, showed that we do possess the letter to which Mendoza must certainly have been referring—a letter written to him by Mary on the 17th-23rd July of that year. In this letter Mary writes *"Or sur ce que de nouveau j'ai entendu de la bonne intention du dit sieur Roi vers ce quartier ici, j'ai escrit fort amplement aux principaux des dit catholiques sur un dessein que je leur ai envoyé avec mon advis sur chacun point."* Now it is clear that, though these words might bear the interpretation which Mendoza put upon them, yet they might also bear a very much more innocent interpretation. Mendoza must have had some additional evidence to lead him to interpret Mary's language so certainly in the guilty sense. Whence can he have derived this additional evidence? The late Father Pollen pointed out in a note in the *Month* for October, 1903, that this letter was delivered to Mendoza by Gilbert Gifford, who had already on the one hand imposed upon Mendoza and persuaded him of his *bona fide* character, who on the other hand was certainly scheming to obtain just such expressions of opinion from responsible people in the hope that they might later be useful in building up the case against Mary. What more probable than that Mary's letter was delivered to Mendoza accompanied by a false oral comment upon it, invented by Gifford?

Such were Walsingham's games. To what extent Elizabeth was privy to them we cannot tell. She certainly seems to have known the truth of the Parry case, and she knew, of course, that Walsingham was, in general, a liar. But, apart from the Parry case, it is impossible to discover how far she knew the particular truth of the particular lies which he told.

This essay is not concerned with a general estimate of the vices or virtues of Mary, but with an estimate of the attitude of the Government towards the Catholic and of the Catholic towards the Government. I do not accept the romantic view of Mary as a woman who throughout her life was never anything but a harmless and injured innocent. As little do I accept the view that there were a whole number of plots against

K

Elizabeth's life and that Mary was at the bottom of all of them. She may perhaps have been guilty of plotting Elizabeth's assassination (though on the whole it seems to me to be improbable), but all that I am here concerned to demonstrate is that she was not proved to be guilty. My object in entering into the question in as much detail as I have is to show, not the innocence of Mary, but the unscrupulous determination of the Government to obtain a verdict against the leading Catholic of the time and its utter carelessness whether that verdict was just or unjust. This, I think, the records of Mary's trial amply show.

The trial itself was a farce. Walsingham himself was a member of the commission which sat in investigation upon the genuineness of that evidence which Mary accused him of having forged, or at least of having caused to be forged. Mary was allowed no counsel. She could obtain no information of the charges against her and the trial ended, as all know, in condemnation. There remained only the problem of how best to put her out of the way. Leicester pleaded for the superior convenience of poison. Elizabeth preferred assassination—but the problem was to find the assassin. Paulet, Mary's gaoler, was so undutiful as to decline the honour. Walsingham, terrified that owing to Elizabeth's vacillation Mary might still escape and that to insist upon execution might even now be merely to save Mary's life, wrote on 1st February, 1586, to him and to Drury, his colleague, pressing them to accept Elizabeth's invitation. Yet Walsingham's concern was unnecessary. On that very day Elizabeth had signed the warrant for execution. Still determined to escape the responsibility, she had hit on a new plan in which she hoped removal would be effectually combined with irresponsibility. She had a new and raw secretary of the name of Davison. He was not yet a Walsingham or a Cecil at the game. She determined to use him and to sacrifice him.

Of foreign powers Spain alone was much concerned for Mary's fate. Yet Spain could do nothing to help her, nor perhaps could Philip be humanly expected to be indifferent to the fact that, once Mary was out of the way, he became by his Plantagenet descent the legitimate Catholic candidate for the English throne. Henry's III's ambassador, Châteauneuf, did indeed register a protest, but Henry's troubles with the Huguenots made him unable to do anything, and, difficult though it be to estimate his degree of sincerity or insincerity, he was not perhaps altogether displeased to see the last of one who was a member of the rival family of Guise. If only the death of a Guise did not leave a Hapsburg the heir! Elizabeth made the pretence of having discovered that an assassination plot was being hatched in the French embassy an excuse to break off all diplomatic intercourse during this nervous season.

Decency demanded that James of Scotland should make some show of an attempt to save his mother's life and ambassadors were sent to Elizabeth to plead for mercy. Yet James was at the time in the hands of those who were very surely determined that Mary should die, and his own desire to save her life, at the best never strong, was wholly extinguished when Cecil sent to him a copy of Mary's will, found at

Charteley, which disinherited him in favour of Philip of Spain. He did not object to the killing of his mother. To him the first question was how much money he could get out of Elizabeth for not objecting; the second, whether, when the obstacle of his mother was removed, Elizabeth would recognise him as the heir to the English throne. "Though it cannot stand with his honour to be a consenter to take his mother's life," yet Gray, his ambassador, made it clear enough that James would not

> strive
> Officiously to keep alive.

It was, according to Professor Tait, James' intimation that he would raise no objection to his mother's execution which led Elizabeth to abandon the idea of secret assassination. Gray, who, as we have seen, had already played traitor to Mary, was sent to make the protest. He did so formally, but privately whispered in Elizabeth's ear that "the dead cannot bite."

Cecil was determined that Elizabeth should take the responsibility for the execution. Davison was now used to push on the arrangements for it, and on 8th February, 1587, Mary was executed at Fotheringay Castle in Northamptonshire. Though she was denied final spiritual consolation and though her faith was insulted on the very scaffold, she yet died a very brave and beautiful death and protested to the last her innocence of any plot to murder Elizabeth. Whatever her sins may have been, it was not her sins which brought her to the scaffold. Through all the tangles and troubles of the times it is yet certain that the cause of her death at the last, as of her imprisonment at the first, was her refusal to deny her faith. Mary Stuart was no saint, but, if a martyr be one who witnesses to faith even at the price of death, then she was most certainly a martyr.

To some it may perhaps seem a surprising and a bold thing to say that the main charge against Mary must be left unproven. It challenges a strong anti-Marian legend, a legend which teaches that solid, scientific evidence condemns Mary and only a languorous romance can defend her. One main support of that legend is the great Froude, and to estimate its value it is necessary to understand what manner of man this Froude was.

He and Charles Kingsley married sisters, and the two were great friends. Froude had always a very low opinion of clergymen and Kingsley an equally low opinion of historians—neither of which, as Bishop Stubbs wittily remarked, was to be wondered at, since Froude knew no clergyman except Kingsley and Kingsley knew no historian except Froude. A brilliant man, one of the great masters of our prose, Froude was yet incapable of truth. History was to him a dramatic poem, and the dramatic poet, he said, "is not bound, when it is inconvenient, to what may be called the accidents of facts." "*Il n'y a rien qui s'arrange aussi facilement que les faits*" he once quoted with approval from Talleyrand, and the epigram was found as convenient to the historian as to the diplomatist. The facts of history, he said elsewhere, are like the letters of the alphabet which by selection and arrangement can be made to spell anything.

When, therefore, we say that Froude was a liar we do not merely mean that we disagree with his judgment on this or that point, as we might disagree with that of Macaulay or Freeman. Froude, alone, I fancy, of the major English historians, consciously falsified his evidence. Again and again, when he professes to be quoting a document or letter, comparison with the original shows that he is really paraphrasing or making it up, or else the quotation is verbally correct but the omission of some essential qualifying phrase wholly misrepresents the meaning. He garbled the letters which Erasmus had written three hundred years before his own time in his *Life and Letters of Erasmus*. He garbled the letters of Carlyle, his own contemporary, in his life of his friend so that Professor Norton writes, "Almost every letter which I have collated with the original is incorrectly printed, some of them grossly so." He was accused by Dominion politicians of misrepresenting their conversations with him in his *Oceana*. He was, in short, a man quite incapable of honest quotation.

Now Froude professed to base his work upon the Simancas MSS, the Spanish state papers which lay at the Spanish village of Simancas and which up to his day were unedited. It is the discovery of Mr. Chamberlain, a writer as little favourable either to the Catholic religion or to Mary as was Froude himself, that Froude took with him to Simancas this incapacity of his for honest quotation. In Mr. Chamberlain's *Sayings of Queen Elizabeth* you will find set out in full the true readings of the Simancas MSS, of passages from Camden and of letters which Froude professes to be quoting and, side by side with them, the versions which he has given in his history. His inaccuracy and perversion of truth has been shown to be so habitual that, as Mr. Chamberlain fairly claims, it is no longer possible to accept him as an authority at all.

When we come to examine the evidence behind Froude's plausibility and fine writing, we find again and again that his case is built upon the testimony of private confessions made either on the rack or in fear of the rack. Readers of Mr. Lytton Strachey's *Elizabeth and Essex* will remember a couple of brilliant pages on the Lopez case in which Mr. Strachey convincingly shows that such testimony, if uncorroborated, simply cannot be taken as evidence at all. He very aptly quotes the opinion of the wisest of the contemporaries of Elizabeth and Mary Stuart, that opinion, put into the mouth of Portia—

> Ay, but I fear you speak upon the rack,
> Where men enforcéd do speak anything.

Reject such evidence, and all Froude's proofs against Mary Stuart collapse into mere opinion.

It is impossible for the mind to refrain from dwelling on the contrast between the two women in whose names the last fights for a united Catholic England were fought. If one were seeking for an example of the catholicism of Catholicism, of the truth that within the Church there is room for souls of every kind, it would be hard to find a better than the example that the same faith was the faith both of Mary Tudor and of Mary Stuart. In the Catholicism both of the one and of the other were grave deficiencies. Mary Tudor was a good woman. Though a blunderer, yet she rarely performed any action for which she had not the honest approval of her conscience. If we were to accept the Puritan or Shavian test that virtue consisted solely in following the inner light at all costs, we should have to admit that there hardly ever existed a more virtuous woman than she. Yet her Catholicism was not a full Catholicism, any more than was that of her husband. It was a Puritan Catholicism. The faith's privileges of laughter and freedom, the generous enjoyment of the good things of this life, were quite outside her knowledge. All these things that ampler soul, Mary Stuart, knew well—knew indeed all too well. She possessed that fatal romantic fascination which beckons across 300 years and blinds to her faults even those who are quite blind to her virtues. Mary Stuart, the queen of laughter and of tears, was certainly no saint. She was for a time an apostate; she was certainly an adulteress, perhaps a murderess. The great-great-granddaughter of Edward IV, the great-grandmother of Charles II, she had in her a quality of despair, which she inherited from the one king and transmitted to the other.

Edward IV saw very clearly that England could only be saved by being freed from the rule of a clique, but he found after a little time that he could only free her from one clique by handing her over to another. Seeing clearly what should be done and seeing as clearly that it was impossible for him to do it, he abandoned his duty in tired despair and took refuge in debauch. Charles II, sadder still, either a Catholic received in his youth, or at the least a man who knew very well that he ought to be a Catholic and did not dare to declare himself one.

fell into moods of black depression in which, feeling
that he was destined for Hell, he was guilty of outrageous conduct.

So with Mary, a cultured Guise among the barba-
rians of Scotland, people incapable of understanding
the graces of civilised life, jealous blackguards determined to turn to guilt her every innocent action. For
a few fatal months her pride and her love of life broke
beneath the strain. She determined to teach the sour
Puritans lessons even in wickedness. And, as a result,
in spite of all her courage and her endurance, of her
fidelity to her friends in a world in which the very
meaning of fidelity was hardly understood, her name is
still stained with an ugly mark which even romance
can never wholly obliterate. Yet it was perhaps the
reward which God gave to her that at the last she
should die, not for her many sins but for that constancy
to the faith of Christ which lust had once shaken, but
which the fear of death could never shake.

As soon as Mary was dead, Elizabeth professed to
discover that she had been deceived concerning the
plot in the French Embassy. Profuse apologies were
offered and diplomatic relations resumed. She swore to
Châteauneuf that it was against her wishes that Mary
had been executed, that she had never intended the
sentence to be carried out except in case of an invasion
of the country. In order to give a colour of sincerity to
her excuses, poor Davison, who had obeyed her orders,
was imprisoned and disgraced. Cecil at first wrote a
generous letter, pleading Davison's cause, but, repent-
ing, did not send it and substituted a frigid and formal
remonstrance. His only two cares were that Mary

should die and that Elizabeth, and not he, should have to take the responsibility. The signature to the warrant would, he saw, fix the responsibility upon Elizabeth, however she might treat Davison, and he was therefore content that Davison should be sacrificed. He was only glad that she had not dared to sacrifice him himself, for she had found courage to abuse him very soundly.

James, Mary's son, was more crudely silenced. He was given a present of £4,000 and was content.

CHAPTER VII

"ONE of the few crimes that have not been blunders," writes Andrew Lang of Mary's execution. It is a matter of opinion. I should have thought that there had been a good many. Be that as it may, it is certain that the murder was a complete political success. As the *Yorkshire Tragedy*, put it in words that fit the murder of Mary Stuart as well as they do that of Amy Robsart,

> The surest way to chain a woman's tongue
> Is break her neck; a politician did it.

So long as Mary, the rightful heir to the throne, was alive, the Catholic cause was still a patriotic cause. After her death Calvinist James was the normal heir; Philip, the Spaniard, was the Catholic candidate, and it became harder for the Catholic not to feel that he must choose between his religion and his country. Whichever way he decided, the decision was not one that he made with any enthusiasm, and, naturally enough, he was very suspicious lest he should be forced in the name of his religion to fight a war in order to help Philip of Spain to the achievement of political ambitions.

The sixteenth-century Spaniard was not a pleasant person to have for a master. Even Father Persons, the leader of the "Spanish party," was afterwards to say that "God had destroyed the Armada to preserve English Catholics who had already suffered so much from heretics from suffering still worse things at the hands of the Spaniards"; and the general policy of English Catholics had been to "refuse all aid from abroad but desire only just sufficient for the overthrow of their self-styled queen and for replacing her by the other one from Scotland." Philip's loyalty to the Catholic cause had been by no means so single-minded as to entitle him to demand of those who were not his countrymen that they should see in him the inevitable leader of their religion.

The appeal of St. Pius V had not induced Philip to attack Elizabeth. The main occupations of Spain were, to his mind, the defence of Christendom against the Mahommedan and its extension over the American Indians. England's treachery to Christendom, which to our minds seems to fill so wholly the canvass of sixteenth-century politics, was to the Spaniard of the time but an intensely irritating distraction to the main business of European politics. The English played to Spain such a part as that which the Sinn Feiners played to England during the late war. Fully occupied in the Netherlands, Philip was willing to make many sacrifices in order to keep the peace with Elizabeth, just as Elizabeth was willing to make many sacrifices in order to keep the peace with him. Even as late as 1580, when he had at length prepared an armament for the destruction of England, he had at the last moment fallen to a convenient temptation and turned it instead to the subjugation of Portugal. To Elizabeth's unofficial support of the Protestant Dutch Philip had been content to reply with unofficial support of the Catholic Irish.

Yet in the Netherlands, as elsewhere, Elizabeth was far from being the mistress of English policy. Heneage, nominally her representative, defied her instructions and against her will forced matters to a definite breach. When Elizabeth was forced openly to ally herself with the rebels, the maintenance of peace was scarcely possible. From the alliance the Dutch gained nothing. Unofficial financial support was far more valuable to them than the official support of a very incompetent army. The object of such a politician as Walsingham was not to help the Dutch but to force Philip and Elizabeth into war with one another. Yet the court of Madrid had formed a much sounder estimate of the true naval and military strength of England than had the court of Rome, and, even at the last, peace might still have been preserved at the expense of a common desertion of allies, had it not been for the determination of the English pirate adventurers, of whom Francis Drake was perhaps the chief, to perpetuate a state of war which was so enormously to their own financial advantage.

In many ways Elizabethan England was, as has been suggested, like Bolshevist Russia. Just as modern society is based upon the capitalist system, so was mediæval society based upon the Catholic religion. The Elizabethans had broken with the one as the Bolshevists have broken with the other. Both were in revolt against the general morals of civilisation. In the one case, therefore, as in the other, there was the very difficult problem of regulating the relations of this anomalous state with the more normal world. Elizabeth, like the Bolshevists, made promises that her subjects would respect the property of others. But her subjects, again like the Bolshevists, had lost any sense of the sacredness of property. Such promises were then easy to make but impossible to enforce. The recently published *Calendar of State Papers* shows us Elizabeth intriguing with the Mahommedan Turk against European society in much the same way in which we find the Soviet intriguing against European society in China or India to-day. In every country into which it could penetrate Elizabethan piracy was as rife as Bolshevist propaganda has been in our own time. Conservative Governments were at the same time as reluctant to quarrel with it if a quarrel could be avoided. Elizabeth was as ready to disown her subjects as is the Soviet Government to disclaim responsibility for the activities of the Third International. There were piratical outrages, of which a good example is the enormous insolence of the seizure of the treasure which was being sent to Alva in 1568 in order that he might pay the Netherlands army, and these outrages were met by cruel reprisals. The Channel was the first scene of them; afterwards they spread to the Spanish Main. Love of adventure and enormous greed were the two main characteristics of these American buccaneers, and the happy accident of religious difference was often used by the peculiar consciences upon both sides, in order to justify their peculiar conduct towards their enemies.

There was nothing especially English about these

adventurers in the first place. In the early days of Elizabeth's reign, when England and Spain were good friends, their adventures were somewhat cosmopolitan affairs. Witness, for instance, Sir John Hawkins' very curious intrigues with the Spaniards, of which it is not now possible to obtain a certain interpretation, but from which it appears that his main anxiety was that he should be handsomely paid by both sides and then subsequently declare himself the sincere servant of whichever should be found the winner. As he received £40,000 from Philip merely in return for his promise of treachery which he broke, he did not do so badly.

There was about these adventurers a spirit that was subtly anti-Catholic even apart from their beliefs which, whether atheist or Protestant as the case might be—some of them, such as Drake, believed in God—were always wholly anti-Catholic. They were abominably and crudely greedy for money; so, too, were many Catholics, but these men had persuaded themselves—and this is what no Catholic has ever done—that greed was a moral virtue. Cortes, that very great hero, was a greedy man but at least he had the shame to attempt to excuse his greed. Drake was a greedy man, and he sat down and praised himself for it.

The casuistry by which Drake defended his piracy was especially comic. He had begun his odd career in the slave-trade under Sir John Hawkins. This trade was illicit, for the Spanish Government feared that, if slaves became plentiful, the value of a slave would decrease and his owner would consequently have less motive to treat him well. Nevertheless it was profitable and Elizabeth herself had shares in Hawkins' enterprise, Jewel, the Bishop of Salisbury, having conveniently informed her that he had had a special revelation from the Almighty that He would be pleased to see the Spaniards plundered.

The ship in which Hawkins and Drake were sailing had been becalmed on the way across the Atlantic and they had all but died. But, as Hawkins put it, "Almighty God who never suffers his elect to perish" had sent a breeze just in time, and they had eventually reached their destination without the loss of a single life, whether among the elect or among the cargo. As they were returning laden with their gains and also with some slaves "*optimi generis*," they were attacked by the Spanish viceroy and their possessions taken from them. Drake consulted his conscience, and the casuist determined that the loss which he had suffered at the hands of these Spaniards justified him in robbing any other Spaniards whom he might come across in any quarter of the globe. He lived up to his principles.

Sir Walter Raleigh, on the other hand, was more naive. He justified his buccaneerings by a line of argument which, if often acted upon, has not been so often frankly stated. "Did you ever hear of men being pirates for millions?" he asked—a rhetorical question worthy of a twentieth-century financier—and gaily set sail for millions and the Spanish Main.

Naturally such men as Drake and Raleigh were always afraid that the chances of international politics might make it convenient to Elizabeth to hand them over to the punishment of the King of Spain. In order to prevent this they regularly bribed Elizabeth with a portion of their gains; yet, although Elizabeth took the bribes, she hated the piracy, and there was always a possibility that the day would come in which she would venture to hand over the pirates to Philip's vengeance in return for some concession or other that she might happen at the moment to want. It was therefore to Drake's interests to keep relations between Philip and England as bad as possible and, if he could do so, to arouse in England a patriotic hatred of the Spaniard which would make any concessions to him very unpopular. He had a vested interest in war with Spain similar to the vested interest of the bootlegger in Prohibition. Cecil supported him up to a point but after Mary's execution, frightened before the prospect of open war, he began to show signs of turning pacifist. It was too late.

As soon as the news of Mary's execution reached Flanders, that part of the English army which was under Roland York and Sir William Stanley revolted from Elizabeth and surrendered the fortresses of Zutphen and Daventer to the Spaniards. There were always a certain number of English Catholics in the Spanish armies and no one could at the moment tell how widespread the disaffection was. At the same time tales began to be told of the preparation of a great Spanish fleet. It was Elizabeth's policy, while she negotiated for peace, to make sure at the same time that this fleet was not allowed to get into touch with Parma's army in the Netherlands. Francis Drake was, therefore, sent to Cadiz to keep an eye on it. Drake had no intention of confining himself to obedience to the Queen's very tepid instructions. He was possessed of bravery and a skill in seamanship, unrivalled per-

L

haps by any other admiral of the world's story. "Were it not that he was a Lutheran," said the Spaniards of him, "there was not the like man in the world." He had an opportunity, such as might never recur, of destroying the possibility of peace between Elizabeth and Philip. He therefore sailed boldly into Cadiz harbour and destroyed the fleet there at anchor. On his way home he was careful to insult the admiral of Spain, the Marquess of Santa Cruz.

Thus were the two powers committed to a war with one another. Finding himself at war with Elizabeth for these largely secular reasons, Philip determined to wring every advantage which he possibly could out of the Pope's Bull. He applied to Rome; he discovered in himself at this eleventh hour a zeal to serve single-mindedly the cause of Catholic Christendom, of which it would have been difficult to have suspected him in the days when he was supporting the claims of Elizabeth against Mary, Queen of Scots, or alarming the English Calvinists by tales of the dangers to their freedom which a marriage of Elizabeth with Anjou would bring. The human character is a complex thing, and Philip, having taken up the cause of the Bull, soon came very honestly to think that he was actuated by no other motives than those of pure zeal for religion. Yet it is often easier to deceive oneself than to deceive other people, and to his surprise, it was a somewhat sceptical world before which he paraded in all the conventional paraphernalia of a Catholic Crusader.

Nowhere were his protestations received with more bland scepticism than at Rome. The intelligence service of the Vatican was at this time miserably inadequate, and under Paul IV, Pius IV, St. Pius V and Gregory XIII, Rome's English policy had been little more than a long catalogue of miscalculations and blunders. In 1585 Gregory had died and there had succeeded to him Sixtus V, a man, as some have argued, not wholly admirable in character but at least a statesman of a different calibre from that of his predecessors. Whereas formerly Gregory had urged the unwilling Philip on to the enterprise against England, now when Philip was at last eager, Sixtus was found to be more than doubtful. Philip found Sixtus quite unwilling to contribute money to the enterprise until it should have openly shown itself to be capable of success. He threw plates at the heads of his servants who ventured to remonstrate with him, and was so offensively sceptical concerning the integrity of Philip's motives or of his intentions that it was rumoured that he had a secret alliance with Elizabeth.

The society of the sixteenth century was infected with certain grave diseases. It would be a very crude reading of history which pretended that those diseases existed only in the countries that revolted from European unity. The passionate nationalism, which resulted from the popularising of the philosophy of the Renaissance, made its way in one form or another into every country of Europe—even into Spain which of all countries was least contaminated by the Renaissance. There is truth in the epigram that "the South decayed because the North revolted," but it is equally true that the reasons which caused the North to revolt were also the reasons which caused the South to decay. The spirit of nationalism, which was to make Englishmen look on Protestantism as something especially English, also made Spaniards look on Catholicism as something especially Spanish. It is hardly an exaggeration to say that in all sixteenth-century Spain there was but one man—St. Ignatius of Loyola, one of the gigantic figures of all time—who saw and relentlessly fought the danger of this attempt to nationalise Catholicism. It is to this great man's successful demand that his Company of Jesus should not be allowed to become a purely Spanish society that we, all of us, atheist, Catholic or Protestant, owe the salvation of Europe from that chaos into which, if the Church had perished, the unchecked exaggerations of nationalism must certainly have plunged it.

Throughout the Catholic world outside Spain there was little enthusiasm for the Armada, and on its defeat Sixtus, who was very much alive to the danger of thus allowing Spain, as it were, to "corner" Catholicism, contented himself with a remark about "great princes who needed a counterpoise lest they become too powerful." Just as it had been the blunder of the fifteenth-century priests that they too nearly identified the well-being of Catholicism with their own power, so it was the blunder of Philip too nearly to identify that well-being with the triumph of the Spanish monarchy.

English Catholics have always had their very fair share of the silly notion that foreigners are in some way inferior. With them, as with the Pope, there was added to their conviction of Philip's inferiority their doubt of his sincerity. "To defend his money he could presently be ready; but to defend religion he could not be ready," wrote the priest, Wryght, in his pamphlet *Whether Catholics in England might take up arms to defend their Queen and country against the Spaniards*. On the other hand, the Elizabethan tyranny was no exception to the general law, which is so very rarely found false, that religious persecution, if it is sufficiently violent and sustained, is successful in achieving its immediate purpose, however great may be the general moral havoc which it works at the same time. To these causes must be ascribed the very oddly small amount of support which Philip's cause could find among English Catholics.

General talk put the proportion of the population of England which would practise the Catholic religion, if it could get a chance to do so, at a half. Cardinal Allen (as he now was) and others put it as high as two-thirds. It is the fashion of *émigrés* to exaggerate the popular discontent with the government in power, and the first figure is probably more near to the truth, though no doubt those who gave it meant little more than that there were a lot who would turn Catholic and a lot who would not. There was clearly no way of estimating exact numbers. Whatever was the correct figure, all knew that the proportion was sufficient to be able to paralyse any national resistance, should the Catholic army land and the native Catholics declare for it. Elizabeth's ministers, in their panic, tried to persuade her to a massacre of the leading Catholics. The Queen refused. Partly no doubt, this was because she saw that circumstances might possibly arise before long in which it would be necessary for her once more to declare herself Catholic and to seek reconciliation with the Papacy. It was the policy of Cecil and his party to make such a reconciliation impossible, the policy of Elizabeth to leave a way for it always open. As long as the issue was doubtful, Elizabeth was holding her hand. Only when the Armada had patently failed did she go down to Tilbury to review the troops. Partly, too, her motive was, I do not doubt, one of genuine humanity. Unscrupulous in the methods by which she would remove whoever stood in her way, she did not, like her father, care for the shedding of blood simply for blood's sake. Thirdly, her motive was one of mere common sense. It was not possible to massacre half the population. To massacre a sprinkling would be but to compel the rest to declare for Philip as their only hope of preservation.

She contented herself, therefore, with precautions. All recusants who had been convicted were placed in custody. Houses were searched; lists of suspects were drawn up. Yet so long as she did not actually massacre, the Catholics were still left with a motive which might make them refrain from provocation, and they vied with others in their protestations, sincere or insincere, of their loyalty. The Catholic peers armed their tenants in Elizabeth's cause; the prisoners of Ely signed a declaration of their willingness to fight for her. Elizabeth's ministers themselves had to admit that no difference was observable between Catholics and Protestants. "No man appeared to favour the Spaniard; the very papists themselves being no less unwilling than the rest to see their native country in subjection to the ordinary cruelty found in strangers."

The miscarriage of political plan after political plan

had induced in many English Catholics a despair of such remedies, a determination never again to have anything to do with them.

> God knows it is not force nor might,
>   Not war nor warlike band,
> Not shield and spear, not dint of sword
>   That must convert the land.
> It is the blood of martyrs shed,
>   It is that noble train,
> That fight with word and not with sword
>   And Christ their capitain,

runs a popular Catholic poem of the day. Yet obviously enough it would be somewhat naive to take all these protestations quite at their face value. Naturally those who intended to declare for Philip did not sign a memorial saying so. Indeed, if any were involved in some Spanish plot—there is no evidence of any such plot—they would be almost certain to be the first to put their names to memorials, protesting their loyalty to Elizabeth. Of the secret hopes and desires of English Catholics at this time we have little evidence. Certainly it is hard to see how there can have been hesitation on the part of a man who felt sure in his mind that the Sacraments were of Divine institution and that the Anglican was no part of the Catholic Church. In the debates of the Counter-Reformation there was much discussion whether a Catholic owed an obligation of obedience to a heretical government. Whatever be the answer to such a general question, that was not the question which faced the Catholic in 1588. The question was the question of the Sacraments. To the Catholic the Sacraments are of absolute value. He may dislike the rule of a foreigner. He may suspect the foreigner's motive. He may greatly long for the rule of those of his own speech. Yet these likes and dislikes, very proper in themselves, can never be balanced against the Sacraments. Political freedom, national independence, personal liberty, the high delights of culture and scholarship and art—all these have their importance. The Catholic believes that in a free and good Catholic society you will find all these good things flourishing more healthily than you will ever find them elsewhere. Yet in comparison with the Mass they have no importance at all. They are of this world and it is not of this world and, if a foreign government will allow a Catholic to frequent the Sacraments and the native government will not, he must then support the foreign government.

Such reasoning is unanswerable. It is not the reasoning of the mediæval mind or of the Counter-Reformation mind, but the necessary reasoning of the Catholic mind at all times and in all places. Yet only the few see issues clearly, and our problem is not with what the Catholics ought to have done but with what they would have done. It is a problem that cannot be wholly solved. It is impossible to tell what were their real feelings, nor, I daresay, if we had *verbatim* reports of all the conversations of every one of them, should we be able to tell much more clearly how they would have behaved if there had been a Spanish invasion. When a man knows that, if certain circumstances should arise in the future, he will then be faced with a very difficult decision, he commonly postpones making that decision until the circumstances arise. No one was enthusiastic for the Spaniards for their own sake, and the great majority of English Catholics had doubtless not decided which side they would support. Had the Spaniards landed, some would have declared themselves for Philip at once; some have resisted him to the last. The great majority would have waited to see which looked like being the winning side and then joined it. Great numbers of conforming Anglicans would doubtless have done the same thing.

Neither on the one side nor on the other did wise observers venture to predict with any confidence which loyalty the English Catholics would prefer (it had come to it by now that they looked at the problem in those terms). With ludicrous exaggeration Persons, the Jesuit, told Philip that, "all Catholics without a single exception regarded the invasion with appproval. Nay, they even burn with longing for the undertaking." Yet the Spanish Government was always too wise to place very much confidence in the loud promises of *émigrés*. Whether, if the Catholic army landed Elizabeth would declare herself Catholic, whether the people would declare for Philip or for Elizabeth or remain sullenly neutral—these were questions to which no one knew the answer at that time, nor are we to-day wiser than they. For, as is known, the Armada never came to England.

Among amateur opinion in Spain there was unbounded confidence in its triumph. The professionals were from the first very well aware of the improbability of success. Parma, from the soldier's point of view, had roundly condemned the whole silly scheme from the beginning. "The Armada was unequal to the task before it," wrote Medina Sidonia, its commander, from Corunna before it had left Spain. "It was much inferior to the enemy's fleet in the opinion of all experts." The Spaniards missed their real chance—which was to have attacked in September, 1587, when the English were still quite unprepared—and Medina Sidonia and Parma were proved to be right. Thus, through this medley of accident and crime and blunder, Protestantism came to appear to men to be an English cause and the province of England to allow herself to be separated from the life of Europe and of Christendom.

Yet in recording the enormous triumph of Cecil and his policy it is necessary to ask "What beat the Armada?" Protestantism is so vague a word that the use of it obscures more than it illuminates. Catholicism had in England two quite separate opponents, Paganism and Puritanism. At the Elizabethan court, said Harrington the Queen's god-son, "there was no love but that of the lusty god of gallantry, Asmodeus." This lewd but gallant Paganism of the Renaissance was doomed to die because it was built upon the basic lies of shamelessness and the denial of original sin, and came quickly to that end of despair which is the necessary end of all Paganism. Yet it was the master of the court of Elizabeth and gave to the Elizabethan age its atmosphere of adventure. It hated Puritanism more than it hated Catholicism. "I know the Calvinists to be criminals whose desire is to destroy all allegiance to

Princes," Elizabeth had said. Paganism was the extreme; Catholicism was the mean; Puritanism was the opposite extreme. Laughter at least flourished in the brutal and lascivious Elizabethan court. The Elizabethans, though they lost their sense of honour, at least kept their sense of humour. In their Protestantism there was no place for Calvin's hatred of joy. Yet, in order to beat Spain, Cecil had had to make an alliance with the Puritans, and the tragedy of the Armada was not so much that the Spaniards lost as that the Puritans won. As the heavy galleons of Spain lumbered up into the North Sea, there sailed with them the last hope for England of many a lovely English thing and not least —paradoxical as it may seem—the last hope of a free English monarchy. For these new Puritans were to make shorter work of the monarchy than ever the monarchy had made of the Church. The England that spoke the language that Shakespeare spoke was soon to fall before the England that held the faith and morals that Milton held.

CHAPTER VIII

THE CLOSING YEARS

THERE is little more to add. After the defeat of the
Armada Elizabeth reigned for another fifteen years.
And, if we follow the conventional habit of treating
English history by reigns and subdivisions of reigns,
we may call these fifteen years the third of the three
periods into which her reign was divided. It is more
illuminating to look on them as part of a larger whole.

By the defeat of the Armada the Catholic religion
was by no means stamped out in England. The very
violence of the persecution which immediately followed the Armada's defeat was proof of Catholicism's
vitality. At least one-half of the people, it may be esti-
mated, would have still returned to their Catholic duties,
had they been safely able to do so. Nor was the return
of a Catholic government to power put once and for
all wholly out of the question by the execution of Mary
and the Spanish defeat. The attempts at a second
Armada, the debates about the succession, the un-
willingness of James of Scotland to break with the
Catholic powers, prove the exaggeration of such a
notion. Yet from now on, the return of Catholicism to
power becomes improbable.

The Catholics, divided by their own disastrous internal quarrels, ceased to be protagonists in the political

controversies of the day. The new issue emerged, and that issue lay between the pagan Elizabethan state and the new rising Puritanism. The battle, first seriously joined after the wreckage of the Spanish fleet had lumbered off into the North Sea, was to be finally settled on the scaffold of Whitehall a generation and a half after our period ends, and in the new world which that battle created the Catholic remnant were to rally to the cause of the failing monarchy as to the lesser of the two evils. Only in its final struggle was the monarchy to return, in a death-bed repentance, to that faith which it had ruined, returning so late that it could do little more than involve its loyal Catholic subjects in its destruction. To follow out such arguments is beyond our purpose.

The Government had only defeated the Armada by throwing itself upon the loyalty of the Puritans. Though it is unhistorical to think at this date of a united, disciplined Puritan party, of a distinctive Puritan theology, yet there was a Puritan mentality, which it is possible to describe at least by negatives. It would take its religion neither from the Pope nor from Elizabeth, and it rejected atheism even more certainly than it rejected institutional religion. It was Protestant and it was not Anglican. Elizabeth loathed it. Yet for the first time at the Armada the Protestant drum, as distinct from the mere no-Popery drum, had been officially beaten, and, the battle over, the Government had to pay their price to their new friends. The price was the execution of twenty-nine Catholics, against whom there was no longer a pretence of any charge other than that of religion. Lord Arundel, now the leading lay Catholic in England, was condemned to death, and, since the Queen could never overcome her habits of procrastination sufficiently either to cancel or to sign the warrant of execution, he had to live out the last six years of his life in the Tower, expecting that each day would be his last, until in 1595 he was released from suspense by a natural death.

The triumph of Calvinism spread from England into the more important country of France. The Huguenot fortunes revived, and in the treachery of Blois the weak king, Henry III, threw into desperate peril the whole system of Christian unity by the murder of its most central defenders, the Guises, only himself to fall in the same year beneath the avenging dagger of Jacques Clément. The French people declined to go back on its firm refusal of the Reformation, and Henry of Navarre was only able to establish himself on the throne by accepting the Mass. The problems of France were left to that uneasy compromise of Nantes, by which France was essentially saved to the Christian unity but remained troubled within her soul by that weakening element of treachery which has infected her policy from the days of Sully to those of the *Bonnet Rouge*.

There are in history some notable examples of the failure of religious persecution, such as those of Ireland or Poland; yet, as a general rule, persecution, if only it be sufficiently sustained and bloody, is, as has been said, successful. In England, at any rate, it has been invariably successful. The half truth that the English are more tolerant than other people must be balanced by the equally important half truth that they are much less willing to be persecuted. There has never been much persecution in England because there have never been many people to be persecuted, because, that is, there have never been people willing to profess a persecuted religion.

Yet history, full of examples of successful persecution, gives, I fancy, no example of a religion persecuting successfully upon two fronts at once. Hating both Catholicism and Puritanism, Cecil had so far had to reserve the whole vigour of his attack for his more dangerous enemy, the Catholic. Now at last he was able to turn on the Puritan. As was to be proved, he had turned too late. The tracts of Martin Marprelate, "printing over sea in Europe within two furlongs of a bouncing priest," appeared in 1587 to answer him. Their attack was on "the swinish rabble" of "petty anti-Christs, proud prelates, intolerable withstanders of reformation, enemies of the gospel and most covetous, wretched priests." The effect of the Puritan tracts was considerable, yet at that date it did not look probable that the Puritans would before long be strong enough to beat the Government.

A vigorous persecution was begun. Two men, Coppinger and Arthington, went one day to a certain Hackett, and announced their intention of anointing him king—a plan the great advantage of which was that it would save the country from any further disputes concerning the succession, since Hackett happened to be immortal. This Hackett had previously been a man of wild life and a reputed atheist, but in a tavern-brawl at Oundle he had bitten off the nose of a schoolmaster, called Freckingham and "after (as some have reported) did in a most spiteful and devilish out-

rage eat it up." As a result of this singular adventure
Hackett was converted to religion. He now, therefore,
blandly replied to the invitation of his friends that he
had been anointed already, that he "represented
Christ," and that he, Coppinger and Arthington were
forthwith to establish a court at Charing Cross and to
hold the Last Judgment. This they set about doing,
making it very clear in their preliminary proclamations
that the number of the damned was likely to be considerable, particularly among those from the City of
London. "All was in a buzz," as well it might be, and
the Government, seeing their opportunity to strike at
the whole Puritan movement in striking at these
madmen, arrested the "prophets" and hanged Coppinger and Hackett at Tyburn. Arthington, who had
influence, got himself off. At about the same time, of
saner Puritans, one Penry, the chief author of the
Martin Marprelate tracts, was executed, and Udal and
Cartwright were arrested. The Brownists felt the full
weight of that persecuting hand which had been
hitherto reserved for the Catholics.

The result of the increase of hostility towards the
Puritans was a decrease of hostility towards the
Catholics and, consequently, the growth of a very
vocal party among the Catholics in England, who were
for taking advantage of the Government's decreased
hostility to repudiate the Jesuits and the Spaniards and
to demand, as a price of their repudiation, toleration
for the strictly obligatory side of the Catholic religion.
The astute Bancroft, then Bishop of London and afterwards Archbishop of Canterbury, was able to foster
among the secular priests a party hostile to the leader-

ship of Blackwell, the Catholic archpriest, and to the Jesuits. Bancroft was careful to avoid committing the Government to any promise of toleration for the Mass —a concession which Elizabeth was unwilling to make and without which loyalty should properly have been repugnant to the honour of any Catholic priest. Yet for all that he was able to entrap some secular priests, as for instance the preposterous Watson, into expressions of violent and uncharitable opposition towards the Jesuits. The Jesuits, thinking that the Church's cause was betrayed, as indeed it was, replied with as little charity, if with better logic. It was the blunder of this party among the seculars that they imagined that the general Catholic culture would survive even in an England stripped of Catholicism. The wiser Jesuits saw more clearly, and the effect of the anti-Jesuit policy was finally to weaken Catholic resistance at a moment when it might have forced concessions from its divided enemies.

Elizabeth's part in public life was now all but played. Leicester was dead, Elizabeth had sold his effects in order to collect the debts which he owed to her and his place as favourite was taken by his step-son, Essex. The affair was a disgusting one, which even the romantic pen of Mr. Lytton Strachey has failed to turn into a romance and it ended, as all know, on the scaffold. After Essex' death, Elizabeth, defeated by her ministers on all the major questions of the day, gave up the unequal struggle. More and more she allowed problems to settle themselves by the intrigue and mutual blackmail of her courtiers. The Cecils, first the father and then the son, throve on the system. "If the

M

Queen were to order one thing and the lord treasurer another, the latter would be obeyed," reported the French ambassador. After the execution of Essex the younger Cecil saw that, what between her unpopularity and her age, the old Queen's day was now done. He turned from "the setting to the rising sun," as his father had turned before him, from Elizabeth to James of Scotland as forty-five years earlier his father had turned from Mary Tudor to Elizabeth, so that, when in 1603 the end at last came, all was prepared for the accession of James. The cold and uncouth child of Darnley and Mary Stuart came over the border to unite beneath a mildly Protestant sway the two kingdoms of England and Scotland, and the courtiers of Elizabeth made ready to welcome him.

CHAPTER IX

THE ELIZABETHANS AND IRELAND

Owing to the relationship between the two royal families, the histories of England and Scotland in the sixteenth century were so intimately, and indeed so inextricably interconnected, that it is least confusing to tell the two stories as one. The history of Ireland, so different from that of either of the two other countries, demands separate notice.

It is no wilful paradox which says that the most important event in early Irish history was an event which never happened. Ireland was never included in the Roman Empire. She was nevertheless Christian. The England of the Middle Ages derived from Rome all that she had—her faith and philosophy, her institutions, the feudal system, her laws. Ireland derived her religion from Rome but her laws and institutions were her own.

It is in dispute among scholars whether the Bull *Laudabiliter*, in which the English Pope, Adrian IV, granted to the kings of England the hereditary lordship of Ireland, is genuine or spurious. Yet, even if we suppose it to be a forgery, there is no doubt that the mediæval popes felt that Ireland's membership of the European unity was only partial so long as she did not share in the general institutions of Europe, and that the

Papacy looked to the English kings to do for Ireland
the work which, two hundred years before, the Norman
Dukes had done for England. Ireland, in the papal
view, was the property of the Holy See. The King of
England should occupy it, as Lord of Ireland and as
the Pope's deputy, in order to impose upon the Irish
mind the normal habits of European thought. In
pursuance of this policy, to quote the old Irish chronicle,
the *Annals of Lough Cé*, on 23rd August, 1170, "Earl
Strongbow came into Erin with Dermod MacMurrough
to avenge his expulsion by Roderick, son of Turlough
O'Connor, and Dermod gave him his own daughter
and a part of his patrimony, and Saxon foreigners have
been in Erin since then."

The papal policy was to import into Ireland English
families who would bring with them the general customs of Europe, which they would hand on to the
native Irish. Thus out of the two races a single, united,
normal, Irish nation would be created. That policy
failed. It failed for several reasons, of which the most
considerable was the determination of the English to
keep in English hands all the ecclesiastical posts which
they could. This determination was denounced by
Pope Honorius III in 1224 as "destitute of all colour of
right and honesty." Nevertheless a papal denuncia-
tion did not kill the reluctance of the English to submit
themselves to an Irish priest, and, because of this
reluctance, right up to the Reformation the racial
divisions of the island's population were, as a general
rule, recognised in ecclesiastical appointments. Irish
congregations were given Irish priests, English congregations English priests. Religion was the only bond of

union between the two races. With Her philosophy and Her gospel the Church could not but do much towards bringing the two races together. As Mr. Stephen Gwynn concludes in his most impartial *History of Ireland*, the influence of the Church up to the Reformation tended on the whole to the decrease of racial antipathies. Yet for the reason which has been given She did not do nearly as much as She might have done.

From the reign of Henry V the failure of the attempt to Europeanise Ireland was frankly recognised. The English ceased the pretence of exercising their influence outside a "pale" of thirty miles by twenty round Dublin and a few towns round the coast, such as Waterford, Wexford and Cork. Over the rest of Ireland the overlordship of the King of England was purely nominal. There was but one single authority which was recognised impartially in all parts of Ireland—the Church. All education was in Her hands.

The reign of Henry VIII brought two great changes. On the one hand Henry, when he came to claim for himself the whole of the papal jurisdiction, naturally declared himself to be absolute head not only of the English Church but also of the Irish Kingdom. No longer merely Lord of Ireland under the Pope, he now became King of Ireland. He became also head of the Church in Ireland, and that headship meant more in Ireland than it had meant in England. For Henry intended in Ireland not only that the Church should be brought under the control of the State but also that the State should very frankly use its powers of ecclesiastical patronage for the anglicisation of the whole country.

The abolition of the papal headship was accepted by the Anglo-Irish chiefs as easily as Henry's changes in England were accepted by the English people. On the other hand, in Ireland, as in England, the lust for plunder had to be satisfied. All the monasteries upon which Henry could lay his hands were dissolved and, as a result, monasticism and education were banished into those purely Irish parts of Ireland, where the native chiefs for the moment protected ecclesiastical property as neither royal commissioner nor Anglo-Irish noble was willing to protect it.

Henry was even more careful in Ireland than he was in England to avoid any change in ritual or defined doctrine. The first attempts at an introduction of Protestantism into Ireland were made in Edward VI's reign during the lord-deputyship of Sir Edward Bellingham. Protestantism came hand-in-hand with a policy of aggression. Bellingham attempted to extend the area of English influence, and castles were established at Athlone, in order to dominate Connaught, and at Leighlin Bridge, to dominate Munster. In 1551 the saying of Mass was for the first time made a penal offence. The policy of Bellingham was continued by his successors throughout Edward's reign.

Bellingham, a stupid and fanatical soldier, was playing a more important part in history than he guessed. The way of the world is for people to divide themselves into parties according to the most important issue of the day. If there is twopence going begging, they quarrel about twopence, but, if a stake of sixpence is offered, then they forget about the twopence and flock off to fight for the sixpence. So in Ireland conflicts up to this time had been either conflicts of rival families or else the racial conflicts between English and Irish. Bellingham had raised an issue more fundamental than that of race or family—the issue of religion. The old issues did not in a single night yield place to the new, yet from his day to ours the Irish question has been predominantly a religious question. The attempt to represent it as racial, whether that attempt come from the one side or the other, is but the rhetoric of stupid men, unable to distinguish an essential from a fortuitous difference. The Unionist, who portentously demonstrates that this or that Irishman is really of a Norman origin, and the Gaelic enthusiast who lectures on the glories of early Christian Ireland or the cruelties of Strongbow—both show themselves to be possessed of minds incapable of reality. Home Rule, to quote the admirably accurate slogan, is Rome Rule.

Though there had certainly been pre-Reformation clerical scandals in Ireland—the archiepiscopal crozier of Dublin had, for instance, been in pawn from 1449 to 1529—yet the controversies of the Renaissance and the Reformation were controversies which, both for good and for bad, left Ireland quite untouched. When, therefore, Protestantism was presented to the Irish as an English creed by an English lord-deputy, they naturally rallied to Catholicism as to the religion of Irishmen. The papal primate was a Scot from St. Andrews', called Wauchope. This man, one of the great figures of the century, though almost entirely blind, was yet reputed to ride post better than any man in Europe; he co-operated with the Jesuits in the organisation of resistance to the English policy. The resistance was entirely successful; the English were unable to penetrate at all into Ulster, the province in which Wauchope had established himself, and the propaganda of Protestantism throughout the rest of the country was wholly ineffective.

Mary had, therefore, no difficulty in re-establishing the Catholic religion in Ireland on her accession. Yet in Ireland, as in England, she was unable to restore the Abbey lands nor, Catholic though she was, did she resign the new title of Queen of Ireland. The Pope had of necessity to recognise what he was unable to prevent. Mary also continued her brother's and father's policy of extending the area of English influence. Offaly and Leix, which, until the establishment of the Free State, bore the names of King's County and Queen's County after her husband, Philip, and herself, bear witness to the partial success of her policy.

It is impossible to defend Mary's Irish policy, and it would be a dishonesty to pretend that at this date the English Catholics suffered from over-enlightened views upon the Catholic Irish. The policy which Mary pursued was but mild in comparison with what Dowdall, the English, or at least Anglo-Irish, Catholic Archbishop of Armagh, considered the ideal policy—which was to expel or kill off all the Irish and settle the whole island with English. "And truly this is the most godly way of reformation," wrote Dowdall, "and most profitable and commodious, if it might be brought easily to pass."

In 1558 Elizabeth came to the throne to continue the policy of Bellingham. In Ireland, as in England, the new government did not immediately declare its hand. Sir Henry Sidney, the lord deputy, was sworn in with full Catholic ritual. But the change soon came. The Parliament of 1560 restored all the ecclesiastical legislation of Henry's and Edward's reigns. Convocation was deprived of all jurisdiction over heretics, who were to be amenable to royal commissioners or to Parliament, and the formality of the *congé d'élire*, preserved in the appointment of the English bishops, was dispensed with in that of the Irish. Yet it was no more possible to enforce the religious settlement in Ireland than in the North of England, and no serious attempt was made to put it into practice outside the Pale and a few big towns.

Elizabeth's reign was filled by three large rebellions —that of Shane O'Neill, that of the Desmonds, and the joint Desmond-O'Neill rising of the end of the reign. On each of these a few words must be said.

Shane O'Neill was the son of Conn Banach O'Neill, Earl of Tyrone. On his father's death Shane claimed the earldom by hereditary descent, the chiefdom by the election of his tribe. But Henry VIII, when conferring the earldom on Conn Banach, had conferred it with remainder to a certain Matthew, reputed to be Conn Banach's illegitimate son. Whether he was his son or not, was uncertain, but, as Shane explained, "being a gentleman, my father never refused no child that any woman named to be his." Matthew predeceased his father, and the Government, therefore, on Conn Banach's death, championed the cause of Brian O'Neill, Matthew's son. During all the first years of Elizabeth's reign Ulster was laid waste by a war between Shane O'Neill and the English forces under

Sussex. Sussex attempted to poison Shane and to lure him into his hands by promise of a safe-conduct, which he then proposed to break; he resorted also upon occasion to more honourable methods. All were without avail, and Shane had the mastery both in war and diplomacy during the deputyships of Sussex and of his successor, Sir Nicholas Arnold.

Sir Henry Sidney, a far abler man, returned to the deputyship in 1566 and things rapidly took a different turn. Driven from post to post, Shane had to take refuge with his enemies, the MacDonnels, by whom he was murdered in an after-dinner quarrel over the cups. His body was "wrapped in a kern's old shirt" and thrown into a pit. The Governor of Carrickfergus managed to get hold of the head which he sold, "pickled in a pipkin," to Sidney for five hundred marks, and for four years it decorated the walls of Dublin Castle. As Mr. Gwynn writes, "Shane O'Neill was a barbarian, cruel and tyrannous. All the details known about him illustrate his savagery. But he was an efficient barbarian. Sussex, his chief antagonist, was an inefficient villain." Nothing could be more false than the popular notion that there was in these days order of a rough sort within the English Pale and a welter of anarchy outside it. The opposite is the truth. Shane O'Neill in his negotiations with Elizabeth was able to claim that many people had left the Pale and gone to live in his dominions for the sake of the greater security which he could offer, and Elizabeth does not seem to have denied it.

After Shane's death the stage was clear for the trial of the great Elizabethan policy—the policy of "plantations." Of the great Irish families only one could be counted on as really loyal to Elizabeth or at all sympathetic to the Reformation—the Butlers, of whom the Earl of Ormonde was the head. Yet the inconvenience of loyalty or innocence in the accused rarely stood between an Elizabethan courtier and the seizure of coveted lands. Sir Peter Carew laid claim to, and seized, a large tract of land in Carlow, part of which belonged to one of the Butlers. The family was driven into rebellion, and a fierce private war between it and Carew broke out, in which the vilest atrocities were committed by both sides.

The men of Munster took warning. The Earl of Desmond, though he had supported the Government against Shane O'Neill, had yet been arrested for breaking the peace by indulging in a family war with his rival, the Earl of Ormonde. He was sent to London and there kept prisoner for six years. When at last he attempted to escape, he was accused of treason and compelled to surrender his land to the Crown. It was at once proposed to use this land in order to found an English colony in Ireland, stretching from the Shannon to Cork. Sir Richard Grenville, the sheriff of Cork and as ready to do his duty in Cork as we found him in Cornwall at the trial of Blessed Cuthbert Mayne, began the work by assigning to himself half a barony to the west of Cork Harbour. Carew, not content with the gains of Carlow, lodged his claim to a Munster estate as well.

As soon as they heard of it, the men of Munster rose in rebellion in 1569. Irish and Anglo-Irish were united under the leadership of the Anglo-Irish James Fitzmaurice Fitzgerald, Desmond's cousin. "The English and Irish of Munster," say the Four Masters, "entered into a unanimous and firm confederation with him against the Queen's Parliament." Neither Sir Henry Sidney nor Sir Humphrey Gilbert, his successor, was able to suppress the rebellion. Sir John Perrot, probably Elizabeth's half-brother, was in 1570 appointed to the newly created post of President of Munster. He was able to bring James Fitzmaurice Fitzgerald to submission but was wise enough to see the impossibility of the scheme of plantation. Similar schemes in Ulster under Smith, the illegitimate son of Sir Thomas Smith, the diplomatist, and the Earl of Essex, the father of Elizabeth's favourite, were equally unsuccessful.

Of all the chieftains of Ulster "the man," according to Sir Henry Sidney, "that heretofore hath most constantly stayed in Your Majesty's party like a true subject" was Sir Brian MacPhelim O'Neill. When in 1571 Smith threatened to establish the English plantation of Ulster, Sir Brian wrote to Elizabeth for a charter of confirmation of his lands. Elizabeth gave it to him. Nevertheless Smith prepared to seize Sir Brian's lands. Sir Brian, thus converted into a rebel *malgré lui*, attacked Smith and drove him out of the country. Elizabeth's answer was to give to the Earl of Essex authority of martial law over all Sir Brian's subjects and territory. Sir Brian at first submitted, then on the arrival of some Scotch reinforcements took to arms, but later on a second time submitted. Essex received his submission, and in 1574 he invited him and his retainers to a banquet. There they were set upon and massacred. Essex boasted that he killed two hundred. "Brian," say the Four Masters with grim humour, "was afterwards sent to Dublin, together with his wife and brother, where they were cut in quarters. Such was the end of their feast." "This little execution," boasted Essex, "hath broken the faction and made them all afeard." It was the opposite of the truth. It drove them instead to desperation. Essex, by his treacherous capture of Sir Brian and murder of his followers and by his massacre of the Scots at Rathlin in 1575, succeeded in making the English hated without making them feared. The only result of Essex's policy was, as Sir Henry Sidney found, to leave the districts where he had been, "utterly disinhabited."

After the failure of these schemes Sir Henry Sidney was brought back as deputy and it was determined by a salutary reign of terror to make certain that such schemes should not fail in the future. At the same time Sir William Drury, who became President of Munster in 1576, hanged four hundred persons in a year; Sir Nicholas Malby, sent in the same year to suppress a rising of the Connaught Burkes, spared neither young nor old and burnt all the corn and all the houses. Those who were responsible for the terror should not be criticised except by reference to the end for which their policy was devised. Once admit the premise that Ireland must be anglicised and once understand the nature of sixteenth-century Irish society, and it must be agreed that no methods save those of treachery and violence could hope to achieve the end.

The attempt to colonise Leix and Offaly, first made, as has been said, in Mary's reign, had naturally led to bitter conflict with the previous Irish inhabitants of those two districts. At last a clan of them, the O'Mores, had been induced to sue for peace. They were invited by the English in 1577 to come under promise of safe conduct and discuss the details of the terms at the Rath of Mullaghmast. When they arrived at the meeting, they were treated as Essex had treated Sir Brian Mac-Phelim O'Neill three years before. They were set upon by soldiers, who had been secretly concealed about the place, and butchered. Their lands were divided among their murderers, whose treachery received neither punishment nor rebuke from the English government.

In 1579 James Fitzmaurice Fitzgerald determined on another rising. It was to be in the name of religion, and Nicholas Saunders, armed with a legate's commission and a banner blessed by the Pope, landed in Kerry with a force of Italians and Spaniards. Desmond, a vacillating and feeble barbarian, had at first hesitated whether to join the rebellion or not. In the end he decided to throw in his lot with his kinsmen and, in the words of the Four Masters, "expelled the English hirelings and warders who had been in the fortresses and towns of the men of Munster, so that by the end of a month he had not left the proprietor of a single townland whom he did not subdue and bring under the control of his *bonaght* men"—that is, his standing troops—"and stewards. He ordered that the Church and the men of science should be restored to the possession of their privileges, and he re-established the religious orders in their own respective places according to the law of the Pope, as was right." He sacked Youghal, then a town inhabited by English people, with terrible atrocities, while the Earl of Clancar did the same for Kinsale. Lord Baltinglass, who attempted to raise the East for the Catholic cause, gained some success at first but was in the end defeated in Wicklow by the lord deputy, Lord Grey de Wilton.

By giving the command to Ormonde, Desmond's great rival, now reconciled to the Government's cause, Elizabeth cleverly divided the Irish against themselves. The Spanish assistance was inadequate; the Irish were without arms, and the rebellion ended in fiasco. The Spanish garrison at Smerwick was forced to surrender and massacred to a man by Grey de Wilton—an exploit so completely in keeping with the normal customs of that day that the Spanish ambassador did not even bother to protest about it. The poet, Spenser, was among the spectators of the deed and Sir Walter Raleigh one of the officers who supervised it. Saunders perished obscurely in 1581; Desmond survived for two years but was hunted down and killed in the Kerry mountains in 1583 and his head sent to London, where it was set up as a trophy over London Bridge.

Five hundred thousand acres were confiscated by the Crown from Catholic hands, no distinction at all being made between those who had rebelled, those who had supported the Government or those who had remained neutral. The devastation of the war—both that committed by Desmond and that committed by the Government—was such that, according to the Four Masters, "the lowing of a cow or the voice of a ploughman could scarcely be heard from Cashel to the farthest point of Kerry." Of this same country in Mary's reign, when it was under Desmond rule, they had written "there was no need to watch or close doors from Dunquin in Kerry to the green-bordered meeting of the three waters." The English town of Cork complained that, when Desmond had been at liberty, there had been good order in the country; now there was anarchy. Spenser, boasting of the efficiency of his own work of destruction, records of the Irish survivors, that "they looked like anatomies of death; they did eat the dead carrion and one another soon after, insomuch that they spared not to scrape out of their graves. To a plot of watercress or shamrocks they flocked as to a feast."

The rebellion suppressed, a more merciful policy was announced for the future. And perhaps the best way of conveying a notion of Elizabethan behaviour in Ireland is to describe this more merciful policy which, it was suggested, should be substituted in 1583. According to it "all Brehones, carraghs, bards, rhymers, friars, monks, Jesuits, pardoners, nuns and such-like should be executed by martial law." Once they were removed, a new era could be ushered in for the remainder with schools and universities, a fixed police and good government.

The rebellion over, the division of the spoil followed. The new Protestant recipients, who were called "undertakers," often themselves absentees, made no attempt to bring over English farmers. Indeed it was one thing to be a Protestant absentee landlord; after the lessons of the Desmond rebellion it was seen to be quite another to be a Protestant occupying tenant, and it was difficult to bring home to the English agricultural labourers the precise advantages of emigration to South-West Ireland. The Desmond massacres, bloody and indefensible as they were, yet prevented once and for all the establishment of a Protestant peasantry in Southern Ireland.

The "undertakers," therefore, for the most part, merely re-let their land to the old Catholic occupiers. Thus was established the Irish landlord system which lasted almost to our own time. It was, as can be seen, simply a system by which a permanent tribute was levied by the Protestant upon the Catholic. Sir Walter Raleigh, always at hand when land was to be parcelled out, succeeded in annexing to himself forty-two thousand of the distributed acres. Spenser also received a grant, and for that reason changed that opinion upon the desirability of extirpating the whole Irish race which he had previously held. A use had been now discovered for the Catholic Irish. They were able to pay rent.

Ireland did not have to wait long for further outrages. In 1588 Sir Nicholas Bingham, Governor of Connaught, hanged seventy persons at the Galway Assizes and then declared war on the Connaught Burkes for their refusal to attend there. Sir John Perrot, then lord deputy, appointed a commission of enquiry into Bingham's conduct, which condemned him. But Bingham appealed over the commission's head to the Queen and was upheld. Perrot soon after returned to England to suffer a traitor's condemnation.

The next outrage was that upon Macmahon of County Monaghan in 1589. The Government had promised him the succession on the death of his brother, which took place in that year. Yet the lord deputy, Fitzwilliam, then told him that he could only

N

receive the land on the payment of a bribe of six hundred cows. Macmahon refused, whereupon Fitzwilliam had him hanged on a charge of levying distress for debt by force of arms—which according to Irish custom he had a right to do. His land was divided among four Englishmen and "the Irish spared not to say that those men were conscious of his death and that every one paid something for his share." Whether this charge was true or false, it does not seem possible to tell.

This uneasy settlement lasted until nearly the end of the century. Then a conspiracy for revenge was entered into between Hugh O'Neill, the new Earl of Tyrone, Hugh O'Donnell, his son-in-law and James Fitzthomas Fitzgerald, the new Earl of Desmond in the South. James Fitzthomas Fitzgerald was known as the Sugane Earl to distinguish him from the Queen's Earl, whom the Government paraded as the Protestant candidate for the title and whom the people booed out of the country. Munster, in the vivid phrase of the old annalist, was "a trembling sod," and at the agreed time it rose to the rebellion. "Within seventeen days," wrote the Four Masters, "there was not one son of a Saxon alive in the Desmond territories." Spenser barely escaped with his life to die in a London garret, while, in the North, Tyrone defeated Sir Henry Bagnal at Yellow Ford.

The cause of this, as of the Desmond revolt, was frankly religious. According to the report of Sir Thomas Warren, Elizabeth's representative, Tyrone, himself, it must be admitted, no very exemplary Catholic, yet "seemed to stand chiefly upon a general liberty of religion throughout the kingdom." Elizabeth answered that she would as soon "give the crown from her head." For a time the rebellion, opposed only by the folly of Essex, prospered, but when Mountjoy, a more competent blackguard, succeeded to the command, the English were able to gain the advantage of their superiority in armament. A Spanish force, which had landed at Kinsale, surrendered. Desmond was compelled to take to the woods. A price was put on his head but, as Sir George Carew complained, "such is the superstitious folly of these people, as for no price he may be had, holding the same to be so heinous as no priest would give them absolution." Yet he was eventually taken "in an obscure cave" near Mitchelstown and sent to London, where he ended his days in the Tower, concerning his life in which we have but one piece of evidence—an extract from the accounts of the Lieutenant of the Tower, "for James McThomas, said time at £3 per week, physic, surgeon and watcher with him in his lunacy." The people were starved into submission by the destruction of their crops, and by the end of Elizabeth's reign Tyrone had been compelled to make terms. A plantation was established at Derry in Ulster under Sir Henry Docwra on the model of the Munster plantations. Hugh O'Donnell fled to Spain. Of him Sir Peter Carew wrote to Mountjoy in May, 1602, "James Blake of Galway is gone into Spain with a determination, bound with many oaths, to kill O'Donnell." In the next October he was able to write, "O'Donnell is dead, and I do think it will fall out that he is poisoned by James Blake. . . He insinuated his access and O'Donnell is dead. He never told the President in what manner he would kill him but did

assure him that it should be effected." The rebellion
had done little save impress upon Protestant landlords
the advantages of absentee landlordism.

In England the policy of the Elizabethan Government was, as we have seen, to persecute the English out
of Catholicism. The Irish policy was quite different
in spite of the paper-similarity between the religious
settlements in the two countries. "Do not," said
Elizabeth to the elder Essex, "seek too hastily to
bring people that have been trained in another religion from that in which they have been brought up."
There was not, for all intents and purposes, any such
being as an Irish Protestant, and very little serious
attempt to create one. If the Irish should turn Protestant, it might, if anything, make it a little more inconvenient to defend that policy which the courtiers
forced upon Elizabeth. That policy was, under colour
of a transference consequent upon confiscations as
a result of rebellion, to levy a permanent tribute
upon the country for the benefit of the new grantees
of the land. None but an idiot could pretend that
the violent and blood-stained Ireland of pre-Reformation times was a golden country and, unpleasant
and unscrupulous as many of the English adventurers who drifted over to Ireland were, only the
most impenitently imbecile of Irish patriots would
argue that the English were entirely to blame for Irish
violence and bloodshed. Yet the Irish chieftain lived
among his tenants; he shared with them in the great
heritage of religion. Even the adventurers whom Mary
sent to Leix and Offaly, evil as her policy was, might
one day have grown under the influence of religion, as

the Desmonds had grown, to be a part of that which they ruled. Between master and man there was no insurmountable barrier. The society might have developed into that property-owning society which is the necessary Catholic social ideal. The Elizabethan settlement substituted for a bad order, capable of improvement, a bad order incapable of improvement. Henceforth no concession, made by the English government, could ever be of real value, for every concession, being made to a Catholic, was made to a man without legal rights and could be revoked at convenience. The social system could no longer be mended save by being ended.

It is the happy glory of our own times to have seen the final defeat of that evil business which the Elizabethans began. Yet the Elizabethan did less harm to Ireland than to England. In England they succeeded in erecting an opposition between Catholicism and patriotism. In Ireland, little though they intended it, they forced the two into indissoluble alliance, and the Catholic faith has kept alive until our own day that necessary patriotism which but for it must most certainly have perished. Where the Normans might have Europeanised, the Tudors could only Anglicise. Irish Catholicism has, it is true, suffered from a too close identification with a merely patriotic faith. Yet it is to no purpose to blame the Irish for this. For if Irish Catholicism had not survived through its alliance with patriotism it could never have survived at all.

CHAPTER X

In the estimate of that very elusive business, the vague, half-conscious attitude of the Elizabethan public mind towards religion, no evidence is more important than that of secular literature, and of secular literature the most important for this purpose is the popular drama. When we find such a man as Sir Philip Sidney, a man held up to generations of English schoolboys as the very type of Protestant hero, consistently using in his private letters a language which it would to-day be impossible to find in any but a Catholic mouth, speaking, for instance, of Purgatory or of the Invocation of the Saints, or when Spenser, almost the only great figure in Elizabethan literature who is outspokenly anti-Catholic, yet denounces the destruction of the monasteries as the work of "the Blatant Beast of Calumny," the discovery is interesting. Yet, when all is said and done, the evidence of the private letter tells us only of the mentality of the private letter-writer. In privacy he perhaps airs eccentricites which he is forced to conceal in public. The very purpose of the popular dramatist, on the other hand, is to please. Opinions which we find constantly recurring in the mouths of the characters of Shakespeare or of Massinger were, we may be sure, more than the personal opinions of Shakespeare

or Massinger.   They must at the least have been
opinions which were not offensive to the normal
play-goer of the day.   Where those opinions are only
echoes of the official teaching they prove but little,
but, where we find the constant repetition of an
opinion that is in opposition to the official policy of the
Government, we may be sure that that opinion was one
widely held in the England of the day.

Now it is no new discovery that the religious attitude of the Elizabethan drama was very different
from that of the Thirty-Nine Articles.   As long ago as
1832 a man as little prejudiced towards the Catholic
cause as Macaulay wrote in his essay on *Burleigh and his
Times* that—

The greatest and most popular dramatists of the
Elizabethan age treat religious subjects in a very
remarkable manner.   They speak respectfully of the
fundamental doctrines of Christianity.   But they
speak neither like Catholics nor like Protestants, but
like persons who are wavering between the two systems, or who have made a system for themselves out
of parts selected from both.   They seem to hold some
of the Romish rites and doctrines in great respect.
They treat the vow of celibacy, for example, so
tempting and, in later times, so common a subject
for ribaldry, with mysterious reverence.   Almost
every member of a religious order whom they
introduce is a holy and venerable man.   We remember in their plays nothing resembling the coarse
ridicule with which the Catholic religion and its
ministers were assailed, two generations later, by

dramatists who wished to please the multitude. We remember no Friar Dominic, no Friar Foigard, among the characters drawn by those great poets. The scene at the close of the *Knight of Malta* might have been written by a fervent Catholic. Massinger shows a great fondness for ecclesiastics of the Romish Church and has even gone so far as to bring a virtuous and interesting Jesuit on the stage. Ford, in that fine play which it is painful to read and scarcely decent to name, assigns a highly creditable part to the Friar. The partiality of Shakespeare for Friars is well known. In *Hamlet* the Ghost complains that he died without extreme unction and, in defiance of the article which condemns the doctrine of purgatory, declares that he is

> Confined to fast in fires
> Till the foul crimes, done in his days of nature,
> Are burnt and purged away.

These lines, we suspect, would have raised a tremendous storm in the theatre at any time during the reign of Charles the Second. They were clearly not written by a zealous Protestant or for zealous Protestants. Yet the author of *King John* and *Henry the Eighth* was surely no friend to papal supremacy.

This is an important and interesting paragraph, the more important and the more interesting because of its author. So effectively has the Victorian interpretation of Elizabethan history been rubbed into our minds that to deny the Protestant nature of the Elizabethan drama may seem to some almost a wilful paradox. It

is well that that denial should come from a writer as
unimpeachably un-Catholic as Macaulay.   Yet his
judgments require modification.   The Elizabethan
dramatists do not write as men "wavering between
the two systems" of Catholicism and Protestantism.
On the contrary they wholly ignore the system of
Protestantism, paying to it neither the compliment of
agreement nor the compliment of refutation.   Nor have
they "made a system for themselves out of parts
selected from both."   The only Elizabethan dramatist
who made a system for himself was Marlowe.   His
system was made not out of Catholicism and Protestantism but out of atheism and black magic.   But lightly
touched by the Christian religion in any form, Marlowe
retained a slight preference for Catholicism over
Protestantism as the more artistic of the two faiths.
The other dramatists were not eclectics.   They were
rather men with two minds.   Shakespeare, for instance,
"speaks respectfully of the fundamental doctrines of
Christianity," when he speaks of them at all.   The
noticeable curiosity is that a man, who speaks sometimes with so much understanding and respect, should
at others have so completely ignored the comforts of the
Faith.   Take, for instance, the pessimistic paganism of
the great speeches, such as "to be or not to be,"
"to-morrow and to-morrow and to-morrow,"   "Ay,
but to die and go we know not where,"

> As flies to wanton boys are we to the gods;
> They kill us for their sport.

This was the expression of one of his moods, and the
constantly recurring praise of suicide proves that there

was a side of Shakespeare in which he was "more an antique Roman" than a Christian. Every one of the great tragedies shows it. *Macbeth, Hamlet, King Lear, Othello*—in every one of them tragedy is manufactured by creating a situation in which the hero ought to turn to spiritual comforts and then denying him that refuge. You find nowhere in Shakespeare the clear doctrine of Massinger's

> This Roman resolution of self-murder
> Will not hold water at the high tribunal,
> When it comes to be argued; my good genius
> Prompts me to this consideration. He
> That kills himself to avoid misery, fears it
> And at the best shows but a bastard valour.
> This life's a fort committed to my trust.

Let us investigate a little more closely this most fascinating subject, the mind of Shakespeare. It is important that we do not argue the matter too pettily. Every religion always survives as expletive long after it has perished as a faith, and, although it is certainly true that when in *Pygmalion* Mr. Shaw makes Eliza Doolittle use the word "bloody" on the stage, he is reminding England of her Catholic past, yet it would be a mistake to make too much of that reminder. So, though it is true that the oaths which Shakespeare puts into the mouths of his characters are all Catholic oaths, yet that is evidence of the creative vigour of the Faith rather than of Shakespeare's own adherence to it.

Let us rather examine what Macaulay has called Shakespeare's "partiality for Friars," and contrast it with his indifference towards the new Elizabethan clergymen. He only puts upon his stage three of such clergymen—Sir Hugh Evans in the *Merry Wives of Windsor*, Sir Nathaniel in *Love's Labour's Lost* and Sir Oliver Martext in *As You Like It*. Of these three Sir Hugh Evans and Sir Nathaniel are mere figures of fun. Shakespeare, who nowhere creates a buffoon priest, does not hesitate to create a buffoon parson. In the precise tenets of Sir Hugh Evans' Protestantism he is no more interested than he is in the precise tenets of Malvolio's Puritanism. Sir Oliver Martext does not appear on the stage long enough to earn a character of his own. He is merely called up to celebrate the wedding of Touchstone and Audrey. The wedding does not then take place; instead of it there is held this most interesting conversation.

JACQUES. And will you, being a man of your breeding, be married under a bush like a beggar? Get you to church, and have a good priest that can tell you what marriage is; this fellow will but join you together as they join wainscot; then one of you will prove a shrunk panel and, like green timber, warp, warp.

TOUCHSTONE (*aside*). I am not in the mind but I were better to be married of him than of another: for he is not like to marry me well; and not being well married, it will be a good excuse for me hereafter to leave my wife. . . .

SIR OLIVER. 'Tis no matter: ne'er a fantastical knave of them all shall flout me out of my calling."

There is but one possible interpretation of this passage. In the opinions both of Touchstone and Jacques a marriage before an Elizabethan clergyman was no marriage and such a clergyman was no "good priest." It is not therefore surprising that at the end of the play, when the wedding does come off, Sir Oliver is quite forgotten in the grotesque exuberances of the masque of Hymen, nor is it by him nor by a colleague of his that the usurping duke is converted from his evil ways, but by "an old religious man," by whom he

> was converted
> Both from his enterprise and from the world.

Contrast with such unceremonious treatment the language in which Shakespeare speaks of friars. It is in the first place noticeable that he is not content merely to call them priests, which would have left it perhaps uncertain whether they were of the Catholic or of the Elizabethan Church. Irrelevant though it is for his dramatic purposes, yet he is again and again careful to call them friars. When the priest in *Hamlet* is to be abused by Laertes for not allowing Ophelia a requiem and the grave-diggers are to hint that but for her father's money she would not have had Christian burial at all, it is a secular priest whom Shakespeare sets up as the target for attack. But for the friends of the good Duke Vicentio in *Measure for Measure* he chooses Friar Thomas and Friar Peter; Francisca, the nun, is the support of Isabella. In *Much Ado About Nothing* it is the friar who by his wisdom saves Hero from injustice and without whom all agree that the final marriages will not be marriages. In *Romeo and Juliet* the

Franciscan, Friar Laurence, is the unswerving friend of hero and heroine and, improbable as his character is from the artistic point of view, yet there can be no doubt of Shakespeare's sympathies with him.

So remarkable indeed is Shakespeare's "partiality for Friars," and indeed the partiality of Elizabethan literature in general, that one cannot but contrast with a wry smile the love of friars shown by those who lived in a friarless England with the much more critical cynicism of a pre-Reformation and Catholic poet such as Chaucer or the coarse anti-clericalism of Henry VIII's reign which we find in John Heywood's *John, Tyb and the Curate*, pious Catholic as its author was. How much the literary reputation of monasticism owed to the dissolution of the monasteries!

> For it so falls out
> That what we have we prize not to the worth,
> Whiles we enjoy it; but, being lacked and lost,
> Why, then we rack the value, then we find
> The virtue that possession would not show us,
> Whiles it was ours.

It is in fallen human nature that there must be authority but that those who wield authority will grow insolent and abuse it. It is the constant duty of the governed to be in protest against that insolence . . . Chaucer in his day was in protest against the real tyranny of the clerical state. Yet, as he would doubtless have agreed, any man was foolish who imagined that human nature would be mended by the substitution of the rule of the Merchant and the Shipman for that of the Monk and the Frere. Such, nevertheless, was the

silly simplification at which the sixteenth century
jumped and it was, therefore, left to Shakespeare, two
hundred years after Chaucer, to protest against the
much greater tyranny of the laic state.

The Catholic Church is not a society for praising
priests, and to show that Shakespeare had a "partiality"
for friars is not at all to show that he had in him any
sympathy for Catholic truth. Many of my atheist
friends have a great fondness for meeting priests.
What is important is to marshall the evidence, not
that he thought that priests were nice men — which
they very frequently are not—but that he thought that
they were priests, that they had certain God-given
powers which neither Elizabethan clergymen nor any
other men possess. There is, as has been shown, striking evidence of this. Remarkable, too, is the readiness
with which, whenever Shakespeare talks about religion,
he talks about it in a Catholic language. He shows, it is
true, a familiarity with the language of the new
Protestant Bible, but apart from that he seems to have
been utterly untouched by Protestantism. The Thirty-
Nine Articles had told the English nation that "the
Romish doctrine concerning Purgatory, Pardons,
Worshipping and Adoration, as well of Images as of
Relics, and also Invocation of Saints, is a fond thing
vainly invented, and grounded upon no warranty of
Scripture but rather repugnant to the Word of God."
"There are two sacraments," they had taught, "or-
dained of Christ our Lord in the Gospel, that is to say,
Baptism and the Supper of the Lord. Those five com-
monly called sacraments, that is to say, Confirmation,
Penance, Orders, Matrimony and Extreme Unction, are

not to be counted for Sacraments." "The Sacrifices of Masses" were "blasphemous fables and dangerous deceits." Yet for all that, Shakespeare makes Juliet go to confession to Friar Laurence; and Paris takes it as a matter of course that she should do so. Romeo draws a metaphor from Purgatory which would be meaningless to anyone to whom the doctrine was not a reality, while, as Macaulay shows, the evidence from *Hamlet* is even stronger than that from *Romeo and Juliet*. The Ghost comes directly from Purgatory. His complaint against his murderer is that he was sent to his account

Unhousel'd, disappointed, unaneled,—

that is, without the sacraments of Communion, Penance and Extreme Unction. Hamlet bids Ophelia get to a nunnery, as to the reasonable refuge from the world. He is careful to tell the King of England to put Rosencrantz and Guildenstern to death at once, "not shriving time allowed." The priest refuses "to sing a requiem" for Ophelia.

It has been argued that Shakespeare's acquaintance with Catholic practices cannot have been more than superficial because in *Romeo and Juliet* he speaks of "evening-mass." He has the laugh on his critics. In the Middle Ages Mass was sometimes said in the evening and it was shown seventy years ago by Richard Simpson in an article in the *Rambler* that—by what is at the least an amazingly interesting coincidence—Verona, where the scene of *Romeo and Juliet* is laid, happened to be one of the places where this custom of evening-mass existed.

A careful examination could, I believe, find striking Catholic phrases in every play of Shakespeare and prolong such a list as this for many pages. Yet the evidence does not, I admit, prove that Shakespeare was a crypto-Catholic. He used the language which came to his hand, even as he used the plots and characters which came to his hand. Only the very rash would speak with confidence upon the true opinions of that fascinating and mysterious man. The evidence that he "died a papist" is strong; we have for it the word of the strongly anti-Catholic Archdeacon of Saperton, who wrote at the end of the seventeenth century and who had, as far as can be seen, absolutely no motive for making such an admission if it were not that he was compelled to it. But it is my impression, for what is is worth, that during the vigour of his life the pagan in him outweighed the Christian. May he not have been like so many of the wisest of mankind to whom the gift of faith has been denied? These men may perhaps receive that great gift at the last; but for the moment they lack it. Yet they have the wisdom to know that they lack a precious thing. They do not, like the empty pagan, pride themselves upon having outgrown the need for religion. They want the Faith to be true. It "has their vote to be so if it can," as Bishop Blougram put it, and they therefore rejoice at the triumphs of the Church; they are shocked at the crudity of Her opponents; their intellect prefers Her appeal to reason to the demand which others make for a blind submission. Yet at the last resort, if you ask them "Do you believe that all these things really happened—that God became Man, that He was slain, that He rose again, that you receive Him in the sacraments?"—they have to admit the failure of their imagination, to admit that they

are not able to believe. Critics have sometimes thought
to find in "the melancholy Jacques" Shakespeare's
own picture of himself, or at the least of one aspect of
himself. If there be any truth in that fancy, then
perhaps with those last strange words with which he
takes Jacques from the stage Shakespeare went as far
as he cared to go along the Catholic road.

> To him will I; out of these convertites
> There is much matter to be heard and learn'd.

He will investigate, though he cannot believe. As for
the world,

> So to your pleasures;
> I am for other than for dancing measures.

It was in this mood perhaps, that he learnt that
familiarity with the devotional poetry of Blessed
Robert Southwell which he is generally admitted to
have possessed. He was probably not a Catholic; he
was certainly not a Protestant.

I have spoken only of Shakespeare's approach to
religion, in the most strict sense of the word. What of
his attitude towards those political consequences of
religion, with which in the sixteenth century religion
was so intimately connected? "Yet the author of
King John and *Henry the Eighth*," says Macaulay, "was
surely no friend to papal supremacy." It is important
not to confuse the two very different phrases—"friend
to the Pope" and "friend to papal supremacy."
Ever since the Hundred Years' War, it had been very
common for the English Catholic to look upon the
Pope at one and the same time as the Vicar of Christ

o

and as an unpleasant and interfering old gentleman.
Dangerous as such an attitude was and proved itself
to be, yet it was not in itself incompatible with the most
strictly orthodox Catholicism.   If a man held such
opinions, he had every motive for publishing them
upon the stage, and it might have been expected that
Shakespeare, a man of Catholic sympathies but not a
Catholic, would have shared the national dislike for the
Italian bishop.   He may have done so, but at least it is
remarkable how little he displayed it.

Macaulay points to the example of *King John*.   Now
King John is a far more extraordinary play than is
understood by those who take it as an example of a
patriotic Englishman's antipapalism.   It was written, it
seems, in 1594—at any rate, well in Elizabeth's reign
and not long after the defeat of the Spanish Armada.
The parallels between John and Elizabeth were sufficiently obvious, the temptation to exploit them large,
and in that fine scene at the beginning of the third act
John defies the Pope, and Pandulph, the papal legate,
excommunicates John, with arguments so similar to
those used by Elizabeth and by St. Pius V or Cardinal
Allen that the similarity must have been conscious and
designed.   So far our lecturers take us.   But it is even
more important to note that Shakespeare leaves out
all the coarse raillery against the Church which he
found in the *Troublesome Reign of King John*, the original
play from which he was copying, and that John's
Elizabethan defiance of the Pope after a flash in the
pan of success ends in complete fiasco, that Philip
Augustus and Louis of France, who show themselves
equally indifferent to the interest of the Church, fare

no better than John, and that in the fifth act John only keeps his throne by completely submitting to the Papacy on all the points in dispute.

Pandulph is not, it is true, a wholly pleasant character. It is a very cold-blooded diplomatist who explains to Prince Louis how he will certainly gain from John's capture of Arthur since John will then be sure to murder Arthur and thus put an inconvenient rival out of the way. Yet Elizabeth did not wish her enemies to be portrayed as unpleasant but as defeated, and Pandulph emerges completely victorious. One of the most trite of quotations is that from the Bastard's speech at the end of the play in which he says that:

> This England never did (nor never shall)
> Lie at the proud foot of a conqueror
> But when it first did help to wound itself.
> Now these her princes are come home again,
> Come the three corners of the world in arms
> And we will shock them; naught shall make us
> rue,
> If England to herself do prove but true.

When had England helped to wound herself? When the barons had revolted against John owing to his quarrel with the Papacy. How was she now proving true to herself? By her return to her Roman obedience. How often do those who use this quotation know the history to which it refers?

The only other piece of political philosophising in the play is that in which Salisbury reflects how much better it would be if the two Christian armies were to stop fighting one another and unite against the infidel—a

very wholesome lesson to teach the politicians of sixteenth-century Europe.

The next king upon whom Shakespeare wrote a play
was Richard II. In that play there appears a shadowy
Abbot of Westminster who plays a small part upon the
King's side. The only ecclesiastic who is at all promi-
nent is the Bishop of Carlisle. He supports Richard
against the Lancastrians, and Shakespeare puts into his
mouth the impressive speech of prophecy of the evils
which are to come to England through the overthrow
of the monarchy. Yet even such a man as Henry
Bolingbroke is made to recognise in the Bishop an
honourable opponent.

> For though mine enemy thou hast ever been,
> High sparks of honour I in thee have seen,

he says in pardoning him.

With the coming of the Lancastrian kings Shakespeare introduces us to a very different type of church-
man. Archbishop Scroop in *Henry IV* is a conspirator
against the King who differs nothing in character from
his fellow lay conspirators. *Henry V* opens with a
dialogue between the Archbishop of Canterbury and
the Bishop of Ely in which the two, fearful that Parliament is intending to pass laws to deprive them of their
enormous wealth, agree to involve the King in war with
France in order to distract the public mind from clerical
abuses. In *Henry VI* Cardinal Beaufort is the villain—
and one of the most loathsome of all villains.

What can we say to all this? Very little. Shakespeare's tale of the "black despair" of Beaufort on his
death-bed is certainly unhistorical. Beaufort was a

better man than Shakespeare made him out to be, and
Scroop was by no means merely the political church-
man whom Shakespeare shows us. To Chichele,
Henry V's archbishop, he was also unjust. As Bishop
Stubbs has shown, "Chichele did not sit as archbishop
in the Leicester parliament," where the decision for war
was taken. Yet, whether or not he was unfair to
individuals, we cannot but admit that Shakespeare was
substantially right in refusing to see in the Lancastrian
ecclesiastic more than a rich, and probably unscrupulous, politician. As has been already said, the higher
clergy were more and more coming, under pretence of
defending the Church, to a defence of little more than
their own financial privileges. Clericalism, in that sense
of the word, Shakespeare hated after the Reformation,
just as Chaucer hated it before the Reformation—hated
it, indeed, just as the Catholic Church has always hated
it. The cry of the Church is like that of the angry man
against the wicked cardinal in Nat Lee's tragedy,

> Stand back, and let me mow this poppy down,
> This rank red weed that spoils the Church's corn.

There remains only *Henry VIII*. It is not certain
what parts of *Henry VIII* are by Shakespeare and what
parts by Fletcher or others. Yet, if we take it as it
stands, is Macaulay justified in quoting it as evidence
that Shakespeare was no friend to the papal supremacy? Wolsey, it is true, is the villain, though, unlike
Beaufort, he learns repentance at the end. Cranmer
and Cromwell are given characters more pure than
strict history will allow. Yet the critics are generally
agreed that their characters were the work not of

Shakespeare but of Fletcher. However that maybe, it is hardly to be expected that Shakespeare should openly declare himself upon the papal side. Yet what is surely remarkable is the avoidance by any of the characters of any discussion of the papal claims. Vague hints about Lutheranism are thrown to and fro and allowed to drop. We are told of the story of the annulment, but told it in such a way that Henry cuts no very creditable figure. Katharine of Aragon is the heroine. "The meek sorrows and virtuous distress of Katharine have furnished some scenes," says Johnson, "which may be justly numbered among the greatest efforts of tragedy." A laudatory speech at Elizabeth's birth is put into the mouth of Cranmer, but her sister, Mary, is referred to with equal respect. Our credulity is perhaps strained when we are told of the wisdom, the mercy, the virtue of Henry. Yet at the same time there is no picture at all of "the majestic lord who burst the bonds of Rome."

There can be no purpose in leading the reader through an exhaustive study of the Elizabethan drama, in extracting from it every phrase or passage which betrays Catholic culture. I am not seeking to prove a universal, to show that that culture is stamped upon every single line that was written by the Elizabethan or Jacobean dramatists, but am merely concerned to show that its influence was widely felt. Yet it is well to re-emphasise Macaulay's point that Shakespeare was no isolated exception.

Macaulay refers us to Ford's " '*Tis a Pity She's a Whore*"—an amazing play, as remarkable for its Catholicism as for its indecency. In dramatic power it is inferior to nothing in Shakespeare or in the Greek drama. Its theme is the unnecessarily repellent one of incestuous love between brother and sister. Yet, intolerably perverted though the problem which he sets himself is, Ford never doubts that the only solution of that problem is the traditional solution—the solution that this is temptation to sin, that sin must be resisted, that the punishment of sin is Hell—and he is careful to put the expression of that solution into the mouth of a Catholic priest. From his amazing riot of debauchery and perversion Ford emerges with the lesson that:

> All human worldly courses are uneven;
> No life is blessed but the way to Heaven.

Take again Marlowe. He was certainly no Catholic. Indeed the defiance of the Pope which he puts into the mouth of Edward II is, with the exception of Dekker's feeble *Whore of Babylon*, the only piece of writing in all Elizabethan drama which sounds as if it were written by a Protestant. Yet in the *Jew of Malta*—a preposterous play considered dramatically—he makes the Catholics his heroes and writes as if vows of chastity and of obedience were things whose validity society took for granted. As for his own religious opinions, it is probable that the strong tradition of his atheism is true, and, if we may accept, as Mr. Havelock Ellis convincingly does, Richard Bame's charges against him, then it was his belief "that, if there be any God or good religion, then it is in the Papists, because the service of God is performed with more ceremonies, as elevation of the mass, organs, singing men, shaven crowns, etc. That all Protestants are hypocritical asses."

Next take Massinger. His Catholic sympathies are so pronounced—especially in the *Virgin Martyr*, the *Maid of Honour* and *Renegado*—that critics have generally admitted that he must himself have been a believing and practising Catholic. The *Maid of Honour* is a panegyric on the excellence of celibacy for the sake of the Gospel. The *Virgin Martyr*, in a professed study of the relations between the Church and the Pagan Roman Empire contains what cannot be but a thinly veiled commentary on the sufferings of Catholics at the hands of the Elizabethan and Jacobean state.

Renegado is a play more interesting still. Its tone is deeply Catholic and Massinger seems to have gone out of his way to praise those parts of Catholic practice or faith which the Anglican settlement had repudiated. "Let us concentrate on what Catholics and Protestants hold in common" is a popular cry of the day. "Let us concentrate on the parts of Catholicism which Protestants have repudiated" seems to have been Massinger's motto. The veneration of relics is spoken of with deep respect and deep intellectual comprehension. The elevation of the Host—which under Elizabeth had been looked upon as the very test of vision between Catholic and Anglican practice—is yet called by Massinger "the work of grace." An insult to the elevated Host is "a deed deserving death with torture." Confession to a priest and the receipt from him of absolution are shown upon the stage, and the penitent is made to utter, as his act of contrition, the beautiful lines:

> Show me true Sorrow,
> Arm'd with an iron whip, and I will meet
> The stripes she brings along with her, as if
> They were the gentle touches of a hand
> That comes to cure me.   Can good deeds redeem
>   me?
> I will rise up a wonder to the world.

He outdoes even Shakespeare. Not content with the depiction of virtuous friars, he quite unnecessarily makes Francisco, his good priest, a Jesuit, and in a play that was performed with applause by "the Queen's servants" at a date at which popular history teaches us that Englishmen knew nothing of Jesuits save that they taught the evil maxim that "the end justifies the means," Massinger yet puts into the mouth of Francisco, the Jesuit, the crowning moral of his play, which is that:

> They steer not a right course, nor traffic well
> That seek a passage to reach Heaven through
>   Hell.

Ben Jonson, again, was in and out of the Catholic Church. He certainly practised as a Catholic for twelve years. Enough has been said to show the enormous strength of Catholic ideas on the Elizabethan and Jacobean stage. It will be answered, perhaps, that the argument does not prove as much as it pretends to prove, since the dramatists would naturally have what would later have been called High Church sympathies owing to the hostility of the Puritans to the stage. I do not deny that there is some force in that argument. Yet it is surely fair to push the question one stage further back and ask "Why was it that the Puritans demanded the suppression of the drama?" Modern apologists for the Puritans, such as Dean Inge in his pamphlet on *Protestantism*, have been keen to argue that the Puritans had by no means that unvarying hostility towards all art with which they have sometimes been credited. I think that these apologists have shown that they have a certain amount to say for themselves. But, if we admit their case, we have surely the right then to throw upon them the obligation of explaining why the Puritans concentrated in hostility of such especial virulence against the stage. There is nothing obviously wicked about the stage. The answer is surely clear. The stage was the popular Press and popular platform of the day. It loathed Puritanism, as public opinion loathed it, and it gave expression to that loathing. Therefore Puritanism, which was from first to last profoundly unpopular and undemocratic, demanded its suppression, just as the Austrian Government would have demanded the suppression of an Italian nationalist paper in Milan in the second quarter of the last century.

CHAPTER XI

THE EFFECTS OF THE MONSTROUS REGIMENT

SOME Catholics, speaking of the Elizabethan Government, begin by condemning its religious policy but then turn and echo a conventional panegyric upon the age and the England of that time; they say to us, "after all, Queen Elizabeth was the maker of modern England," or some words of the sort. Again, other Catholics speak as if, had Mary, Queen of Scots, succeeded to the throne, all modern England would have been exactly as it is to-day except only that everybody would have gone to Mass. It is important, therefore, that we try to form an estimate of the probable effect upon our lives, had the great Elizabethan experiment failed.

The Catholic faith, as all history shows, brings to the country which professes it a large number of secondary and social benefits. Yet these benefits are only secondary. Her business is not with this world and Her promises are not for this world. I could imagine a man saying, "Politically speaking, the Reformation was a blessing. As a result of it, we are to-day the freest, the happiest and the richest people in the world. To it is due our superiority over those foreign nations which had no Reformation. Nevertheless those advantages are never to be set against the disaster of the loss of the Mass." Such a man would be a refreshingly logical thinker. Yet he would at the same time be an ill-read historian.

Before entering upon an examination such as that which I have proposed, it is first necessary to get the mind clear upon one large preliminary obstacle. What is the meaning of the language of rhetoric in which it is to-day so common to talk about the Elizabethan age? "England then truly great"—"a race of immortals"—"made us a nation"—"the spacious times of great Elizabeth"—"Drake and Hawkins, Raleigh and Frobisher"—what does it all amount to? What do we owe to the Elizabethans?

Elizabethan literature? It is true. The nationalism of the Renaissance was the cause of two effects, the one good and rational, a national literature, the other bad and irrational, a national religion (if the phrase "national religion" be not a contradiction in terms).

The first foundations of our empire? Strictly the claim is false. Such men as Drake were not empire-builders. They made no attempt to rob Spain of her territory nor to annex it to England. Their spirit, for good or bad, had very little in common with the spirit which has built and maintained our great commercial empire. Raleigh's colony of Viginia was a fiasco and had to be abandoned. The surviving American settlements are all of Stuart foundation. Yet it is certainly true that interest in America dates from the Elizabethan era. It was natural for such a country as England to exploit the new discovery of America. The only wonder was that she was so slow in doing so and allowed other nations to get so large a start on her. In any case there would doubtless have been plenty of good English pirates to prey upon the Spanish galleons, but the happy accident of religious difference certainly gave a zest to that piracy which it would otherwise have lacked. To flout the papal decision which divided the New World between Spain and Portugal became a patriotic and religious duty.

The world has seen many viler deeds than those of the Elizabethan pirates. Yet at the same time, if they were not abominably vicious, it is hard to understand how anyone can pretend to find them excessively virtuous nor why such men should be held up to us, as no others in English history are held up, as models. We are told that the Elizabethans beat the Spanish Armada? It is true. But Englishmen have fought and won and lost wars in every generation since Rome fell. Why is this one war so especially singled out and those who took part in it spoken of in a peculiar and uncritical language that we are not expected to employ about the men and women of any other generation in our history? It is the fashion to discuss religious questions in non-religious, and therefore false, language and there is no better example of this fashion than that of popular rhetoric about the Elizabethans. Is it not clear that the cause of all that rhetoric is one thing alone? This was the first English generation that had thrown over Catholicism. All other reasons are but pretence. The Spanish war is singled out for praise, when twenty other wars just as important are relegated to the mustiest corner of the text-book, simply because in that war the English cause was more clearly and certainly an anti-Catholic cause than any which she has championed before or since. Of the peculiar institutions of England there is but one that we owe to the reign of Elizabeth—the Church of England. The rhetoric which says that Elizabeth made England means only that she first established the separation of England from the Catholic unity.

Now a man in whose eyes that separation was wholly beneficial might with some show of reason say, "The good that this woman and those who worked with her accomplished was so gigantic that it would be ungenerous if I pried too critically into every detail of their lives. Men, who were so bravely right on this supreme issue, must have had good reason for their conduct in smaller matters, even though that conduct sometimes seems strange to me. They are above my judgment; let me praise instead of judging them." Yet it is muddle-headed to expect such rhetoric in a Catholic mouth.

The Catholic only asks that, where there is a pretence at judgment, then judgment should be passed on the Elizabethans by the same standards by which we judge other historical characters. We demand that it be not considered cheap paradox if a man writes of, say, Sir Walter Raleigh in some such way as this, "He was a man of great intelligence, a good scholar, a master of verse. At the same time it is a gross exaggeration which seeks to put him in the first rank of English statesmen; his major political judgments were with few exceptions quite disastrously wrong. There must, too, have been an intolerable vulgarity in the soul of one who was on the make, morning, noon and night, day after day, as he was. He was far from being the worst of men; yet he was considered false and treacherous even according to the not very elevated standards of his own day. He was certainly not a coward, but there is no reason to imagine that he was phenomenally brave. He was on the whole a bad man."

If we try to keep ourselves free, on the one hand, from the Tennysonian rhetoric, and on the other from a reaction from that rhetoric, which tempts us to see nothing but vice where it had seen nothing but virtue, what can we say of the effects of Elizabethan government upon our life to-day? A book could be written in answer to that question—a book that contained much that was more or less probable and little that was certain. It may be both of interest and importance to make a few suggestions of the kind of England which it seems probable might now exist had the Elizabethan experiment failed.

Whatever the promises of pope or queen, the dominance over a Catholic England of the abbey-land-grabbers would not have been permanently tolerated. In one way or another they would have been put back to their more modest places. Had that happened, the monarchy, with no rich oligarchy to menace it, would, it is reasonable to assume, have been able to survive and to prevent the still further concentration of wealth in the hands of the few which resulted from the enclosures of the eighteenth century. If the monarchy had survived, then all mineral rights would have remained vested in the Crown. Let us suppose that it was in such an England that the discoveries which brought about the Industrial Revolution were made. Those discoveries would certainly have been exploited in due time, but the growth of industrialism would, it is almost certain, have been much slower than it actually was. The floating, landless population, which it was possible to use for factory-labour, would not have existed. On the other hand, the rewards of industry would have been less unequally distributed than they were under the unchecked capitalism of the first years of the last century. If the struggle over the Corn Laws had come up, a far larger proportion of the country's population would have had an interest in the preservation of the country's agricultural system and the Laws could perhaps have been saved. If so, the country's standard of living during the latter half of the nineteenth century would have been lower than it actually was. On the other hand, its development would have been less lop-sided and we, to-day, not being so largely dependent upon foreign trade, should not be faced with our present unemployment problem.

There would have been other differences. Our empire, if developed by a monarchy, must have been much smaller in area. On the other hand, it would have been much more definitely cultural. The smaller empire would have shared more consciously in the English and European culture than do either our Dominions or our native territories to-day. England and Ireland would all but certainly have grown into a single nation and England been spared the disgrace of tyranny and the humiliation of final defeat. The influence on the history of developing America of the survival of the English monarchy would have been so enormous that it is quite impossible to estimate it.

Yet an isolated and insular discussion of the effects of the Elizabethan experiment is to small purpose.

For, if that experiment had collapsed, the effects would have been felt, not only in England but throughout Europe. The Huguenot resistance would have subsided. Spain would have reimposed her rule upon the Dutch. All Protestantism, at any rate as an important political force, would have perished. Christendom would have returned to her unity. The siege of Europe would have been raised. Instead, Europe has remained under siege to this day, and the effect of that siege upon the development of Catholic Europe has been enormous.

The Reformation was, it is true, not the cause but the effect of nationalism. Yet its success stamped national divisions with, as it were, a mark of sacredness. Even in Catholic countries the monarch, in envy of the English Tudors, succeeded in concentrating into his own hands powers of patronage over the Church, and the pious, afraid that the half of Europe which had kept the Faith could not afford to divide its forces in face of the enemy, accepted the insolence of the State with too little protest. That conception of international law, to which we in our terror are now trying to grope back our way feebly and with no coherent philosophy to guide us, was obliterated from men's minds by the cheerful, evil, happy nationalism, of which the Elizabethan State offered the supreme and most successful example. The spiritual unity of Europe was broken in the sixteenth century. Had it not been for the success of the Elizabethan experiment, the attempt to break it would have failed.

I can imagine an objector saying, "How can you be so dishonest as to ascribe all this evil, if evil it be, and

P

the consequences which, you say, flowed from it, to poor Queen Elizabeth? Take whatever period you choose as the golden age of your mediæval culture—the England of Edward I, the France of Louis IX. Can you deny that these societies were filled, as every society has been filled, with falsehood and treachery, violence and shortsighted selfishness?" I do not deny it. By some writers a great deal less than justice has been done to mediæval practice. Still I am not here concerned with mediæval practice. It was, I admit, filled with defects. I am concerned with its principle, with the great question which the mediæval mind set out to answer. That question was, "Granted, as reason demands that we do grant, that the purpose of the creation is the greater glory of God, how can that purpose be best served in every one of the activities of man?" Between us and this great philosophy, between England and the understanding of St. Thomas, stands the decadence of the Elizabethans. The "regiment" of Elizabeth cut England off from the rational, mediæval mind. It completed the destruction of the concept of Europe as a society.

It is quite possible that, had this concept survived and regained strength, as it must have done, from the failure of the Elizabethan experiment, then both the disastrous Continental rivalry of the seventeenth and first half of the eighteenth century between Austria and France, and the long hundred and fifty years of Anglo-French War, which stretch from the time of William III to the Battle of Waterloo, might have been avoided or at the least—and this is more probable—checked in time. Wars, which their participants did not think of as religious at all, would have been impossible, had the religious condition of Europe been different. The Prussian monarchy which rose by using, first, French assistance against Austria, and afterwards British assistance against France, could never have grown to its strength, and the whole history of our time would have been changed.

The survival of English Protestantism, as I have said, put Catholicism under siege. The Catholics in Catholic countries could no longer afford to fight out freely those controversies which are necessary for the healthy life of a Catholic society. The layman on the one hand was robbed of his normal privilege of resistance to illegitimate clerical pretensions with the result that the priests, as men, were insufficiently criticised before the public. On the other hand, the Papacy, afraid that, if it resisted, Louis XIV would follow the example of Henry VIII, was compelled to make the disastrous Gallican concessions—those concessions the envy of which by the *rois philosophes* led to all the Church's troubles in Spain, Italy and Austria in the eighteenth century. Had a healthy criticism of priests been encouraged and had the Church at the same time remained independent of the State, the corruption of eighteenth-century French Catholicism would never have come about nor would the Church have been dragged down with the State's decline. Atheist bishops would never have disgraced Her. And the effect of an uncorrupt Church on the liberal thought of the eighteenth century or on the history of the Revolution it is impossible to estimate.

Man is but feeble and fallible and, if he escapes one

crime or blunder, he soon plunges into another. Even
if England had survived the menace of the Reformation,
something else would have gone wrong. We should
have had troubles enough. There would have been
no golden age. Yet we should have met those troubles
with the idea of unity still strong in our minds. We
should have been saved from the worship of the
Nation-God, the foolish belief that we are a chosen
people and that men on the other side of a strip of water
have souls of a different sort from ours.

This loss of a sense of the unity of institutions and
vocations, this constant mistaking of means for ends
and of the part for the whole, comes from the loss of the
unity in the soul, from the loss, that is, of a coherent
philosophy. Nor will England ever be at ease again
until she returns to a philosophy which teaches her
that the good, the true and the beautiful, are but three
aspects of the same reality, that you cannot discuss
æsthetics apart from ethics, ethics apart from metaphysics, metaphysics apart from religion, that the
state is an organisation of families for their mutual
benefit, that England is a part of Europe. In that
philosophy alone can she fulfil her destiny. For England is a province of Europe and the mind of an Englishman made for reason. It was beneath the "monstrous
regiment" of Elizabeth that the great province of
England was divided from her destiny and that unity
of Christendom shattered, the recreation of which is
the largest social need of our time.

INDEX

ADRIAN IV, and Bull *Laudabiliter*, 177

Advertisement, Written to a Secretary of my Lord Treasurers of England by an English Intelligencer, An, quoted on Raleigh's atheism, 117,

Alençon, Duc d' ,proposed marriage to Elizabeth, 85, 86; and Campion, 108

Allen, Cardinal, founds seminary at Douai, 96, 97; on persecution, 109-11; on English atheism, 117, 118; attempted assassination of, 119, 120, 128; on proportion of English Catholics, 162, 163

Alva, Duke of, and Ridolfi plot, 83, 84; seizure of treasure of, 156

Anjou, Duc d', Elizabeth's proposed marriage with, 83, 84

Annals of Lough Cé, quoted, 178

Anselm, St., on rights of sovereignty, 75

Arden, execution of, 115, 116

Arnold, Sir Nicholas, and Shane O'Neill, 184

Arran, Earl of, irreligion of, 19, 20

Arthington, antics of, 173-4

Arundel, Lord, letters of, to Elizabeth, 116, 117; condemnation of, 171, 172

As You Like It, quoted, 201, 202, 207, 208

BABINGTON, Thomas, plot of, 126, 134-6; and Curle, 139, 140-2

Bagnal, Sir Henry, defeated at Yellow Ford, 192, 193

Ballard, and Babington plot, 134, 135

Baltinglass, Lord, rises in Wicklow 188, 189

Bancroft, Archbishop, and the secular priests, 174, 175

Bartholomew, St., massacre of, 86-90

Bassett, and Topcliffe, 115

Beaton, Cardinal, assassination of, 128

Bellarmine, and James I, 75

Bellingham, Sir Edward, policy of, in Ireland, 180-1

Bentivoglio, Cardinal, report of, 19-21

Bingham, Sir Nicholas, Governor of Connaught, 191

Black Death, 10, 11

Blake, James, and death of Hugh O'Donnell, 193, 194

Blackwell, Arch-priest, dissatisfaction with, 174-5

Blougram, Bishop, quoted, 206

Boleyn, Anne, and gospel-light, 14-17

Bonnet Rouge, 172

Bothwell, Mary's marriage with, 49, 50

Bourbon, Antoine de, King of Navarre, 40, 41; Elizabeth's intrigue with, 42

Burleigh and his Times, by Macaulay, quoted, 197, 198

Burnet, Bishop, on unpopularity of religious changes, 19-21

CADIZ, Drake's victory at, 159, 160

Calais, loss of, 26, 27; bait of, 40-43

Calvin, John, Philip II, and, 32, 33; position of, 35, 36; and Cecil, 36, 37; religious posi-

PRINTED IN GREAT BRITAIN BY
THE   STANHOPE   PRESS   LTD
ROCHESTER   :   :   KENT